W9-AWB-574

STRATEGIC PLANNING GUIDE FOR COMMUNITY BANKS & THRIFTS

STRATEGIC PLANNING GUIDE FOR COMMUNITY BANKS & THRIFTS

DOUGLAS V. AUSTIN, Ph.D.
and CRAIG D. BERNARD

Revised Edition

McGraw-Hill
New York San Francisco Washington, DC Aukland Bogotá
Caracas Lisbon London Madrid Mexico City Milan
Montreal New Delhi San Juan Singapore
Sydney Tokyo Toronto

Library of Congress Cataloging-in-Publication Data

Austin, Douglas V.
Strategic planning guide for community banks and thrifts / Douglas V. Austin and Craig D. Bernard.— Rev. ed.
p. cm.
Rev. ed. of: Strategic planning for banks. c1990.
Includes bibliographical references.
ISBN 0–7863–1183–5
1. Bank management—United States. 2. Community banks—United States. 3. Thrift institutions—United States. 4. Strategic planning—United States. 5. Banks and banking—United States. I. Bernard, Craig D. II. Austin, Douglas V. Strategic planning for banks. III. Title.
HG1615.A99 1998
332.1'2'0684—dc21 97-32838
CIP

McGraw-Hill

A Division of The ***McGraw·Hill*** *Companies*

1 2 3 4 5 6 7 8 9 0 DOC/DOC 9 0 2 1 0 9 8 7

ISBN 0-7863-1183-5

The sponsoring editor for this book was Andrew Seagren, the editing supervisor was Donna Namorato, and the production supervisor was Suzanne W. B. Rapcavage. It was set in Palatino by Carol Barnstable of Carol Graphics.

Printed and bound by R. R. Donnelley & Sons Company.

The previous edition of this book was published under the title *Strategic Planning for Banks.*

This book is printed on recycled, acid-free paper containing a minimum of 50% recycled de-inked fiber.

Rufus P. Austin (1902–1963); Anne Louise Treadwell Austin (1906–1989)

This book is dedicated to the parents of Dr. Douglas V. Austin and the grandparents of Craig D. Bernard. Without their involvement, personally and historically, this book would not have been possible. As their absence continues, their presence continues to be missed even more.

CONTENTS

FOREWORD

Strategic planning is no longer just a buzz word—it has become a serious, scientific, and objective analysis to a financial institution's future. Regulatory authorities increasingly require thorough strategic planning, and the strategic plan is considered a necessity for the survival of a financial institution. The authors of this work hope that use of this book as a reference will improve strategic planning and bring greater financial and managerial accomplishments in the future.

This is the third book I (Dr. Douglas V. Austin) have written on strategic planning for financial institutions. My first book, *The Banker's Handbook on Strategic Planning* (coauthored with Mark Mandula in 1985), was a pioneering strategic planning work for commercial banks, especially community banks. That edition had its evolution back when there was almost no strategic planning in the financial institutions industry. The second book, *Strategic Planning for Banks: Meeting the Challenges of the 1990s* (coauthored with Paul Simoff in 1990), improved upon the first edition and expanded the methodological approaches to financial institution strategic planning. However, time passed that edition by, and although it is still in print as of the date of this writing, many new developments in strategic planning are outlined in this third volume.

I have the pleasure of working with Craig D. Bernard as coauthor on this third book. Craig is executive vice president for AFSI (Austin Financial Services, Inc.) and is one of my five sons. We have worked together for the past 13 years, and he is extensively involved in AFSI's strategic planning engagements for our community bank and thrift consulting firm.

This book, *Strategic Planning Guide for Community Banks and Thrifts,* is designed to assist in a hands-on, how-to approach to strategic planning for the first time (if for some reason a strategic plan has not been undertaken as of yet). The book emphasizes what to do with the strategic plan once it has been created, how to improve the plan over time, and how to utilize tools such as strategic planning retreats to improve the overall strategic planning process and the plan itself.

The authors gratefully acknowledge the research efforts of Victor Wallace, an MBA graduate at the University of Toledo who assists the staff at Austin Financial Services, Inc., as well as the secretarial services of Sandy Incorvaia, Karen Niehous, and JoAnn Parker, who have spent countless hours on the drafts of this manuscript. Without the dedicated, loyal efforts of AFSI staff, the authors would not have had an opportunity to complete this book.

STRATEGIC PLANNING GUIDE FOR COMMUNITY BANKS & THRIFTS

CHAPTER 1

Strategic Planning: The Key to Survival

Strategic planning is the key to survival of a community bank,* thrift, or bank holding company. A ship in open water with a broken rudder will drift in the water with no direction. Even the person who has a choice of two directions at a fork in the road is better off than you are if you haven't decided to develop a strategic plan for your organization. This book is designed to provide a practical guide to help you plan for the future so that you can survive as an independent community banking organization. Affiliates of multibank holding companies will find applications that will help determine logical and rational activities in line with corporate objectives and constraints.

* For the sake of clarity and space, *community bank* or *bank* hereafter shall refer to a commercial bank, a thrift institution (i.e., mutual savings bank, stock savings bank, mutual and stock savings and loan associations, but not credit unions), and bank and thrift holding companies.

STRATEGIC PLANNING DEFINED

The phrase *strategic planning* is a buzz word. In the past several years, many articles have been published on the advantages and disadvantages of the concept of strategic planning. Some authors and speakers want to call it "strategic management" or simply "planning." Others don't believe in the concept at all. In spite of these different opinions, strategic planning is an organized thought process that utilizes the participation of employees, management, and the board of directors. The ultimate result is the determination of long-term goals and objectives and short-term implementation of specific goals using techniques and tactics that permit the corporation to meet long-term goals and objectives. The phrase *strategic planning* is used throughout this book to indicate that planning should be more than haphazard and subjective. Strategic planning should be logical, objective, and continuous.

Regardless of an institution's size, a sound strategic plan is essential for success. In most large banks, managers and supervisors would not be able to operate without clear and precise goals and objectives. Many small- to medium-size banks (with more centralized management) could profit from development and implementation of a strategic plan. Strategic planning is not too difficult or time consuming, and the results of a good plan are easily measurable.

IMPORTANCE OF STRATEGIC PLANNING

Strategic planning is important to the survival of the bank because without it an organization lacks foresight, goals, and objectives. It is the process of strategic planning, not necessarily the result, that is crucial to the bank's future course of direction. In fact, survival may not even be the overall objective. Perhaps the result of strategic planning is to sell out, leave the industry, and pay off the shareholders. Even selling can be an affirmative decision when it is reached after a prolonged and objective analysis. Any decision is better than no decision.

The ultimate goal of strategic planning is the full involvement of management and the board of directors (as proxy for shareholders) in determining the future course of the bank. The strategic planning process compels bankers to examine what will happen 1, 3, 5, or 10 years in the future and whether their livelihoods will be protected and hopefully advanced through the successful operations of their employer. As a part of this process, bankers gain perception of the overall impact of planning upon the operation of their institution as well as insight that the daily problems and overall performance of their department impacts the entire bank. By developing this consensus and by determining the strengths and weaknesses of the bank, the institution will be stronger and better able to cope with the problems it faces.

An extremely important aspect of strategic planning is the involvement of outside directors in the planning process. Since many outside directors are not professional bankers and typically do not have the necessary expertise to run a bank on a day-to-day basis, involvement in the planning process can increase their knowledge of the banking industry. More important to bank management, strategic planning can make outside directors aware of administrative and operational problems faced by bankers on a day-to-day basis. In general, the more directors know of the problems bankers face, the better they will do their jobs as directors.

Outside directors should also be encouraged to incorporate their nonbanking business, management, and community experiences and expertise into the strategic planning process. Assisting management in looking beyond the day-to-day operations is essential to development of a long-term strategic plan. The varied experiences of outside directors should be examined for applicability in the banking environment in setting the strategic goals and objectives of the bank.

Practical examples presented throughout this book can help start the strategic planning process. First-year results will not be perfect. However, utilizing the planning process the first year will help you become better planners for the second year. Mistakes made the first year will become more evident and can be corrected as second-year planning progresses. Strategic planning is a calculated business risk of management and the board of directors. It is an attempt to determine the bank's direction over the next 5 to 10 years through the implementation of specific policies and procedures. Directors and bankers really have two choices: either take risks and plan appropriately, revising plans when necessary, or simply maintain the status quo. If the latter approach is taken, there is no design for the bank's future 6 months or 6 years down the line. Some financial institutions have survived that way for the past 50 years. Unfortunately, these banks will not survive that way today. Lack of planning can put a bank in a position where it must sell, owing to lack of management succession, bad loan portfolios, low earnings, or shareholders who want more liquidity for their bank stock. Any way you look at it, proper strategic planning might not stop a financial institution from selling, but it certainly would provide choices about selling or not selling.

HOW-TO PROCESS

This book provides specific policies, procedures, and examples to assist in preparing your strategic plan. Examples are illustrative, not definitive. Our combined consulting experience has reinforced our conviction that no two financial institutions are the same. The same general approach can be applied to almost every financial institution, but each individual bank has its own personality, character, and way of doing business. Therefore, policies, procedures, and examples used in this book should be used as guidelines and illustrations to be modified to meet your specific situation.

SCOPE OF THE BOOK

This edition of the *Strategic Planning Guide for Community Banks and Thrifts* extends the discussion of the strategic planning process to include annual revisions, amendments, and reapproval. When the *Bankers Handbook on Strategic Planning** was originally published, less than 5 percent of the community banks and thrifts throughout the country had written strategic plans. This third book is being written in an environment where over 50 percent of community banks now have a written strategic plan. However, many of these institutions do not utilize the plan on a regular basis, and revisions to the plan are generally on an annual basis. Many community banks simply update their strategic plan at the end of the previous planning horizon. In actuality, the strategic plan should be examined and revised annually. Thus, the scope of this book not only provides a how-to guide to developing a strategic plan for your financial institution but also provides guidance on what to do with your strategic plan, how to revise it, improve it, review it, and reapprove it so that it becomes an ongoing written road map for the operations of your bank.

The development of the strategic plan will require that you first analyze the bank from a perspective of strengths, weaknesses, opportunities, and threats (SWOT).

---

* Douglas V. Austin and Mark S. Mandula, *Bankers Handbook for Strategic Planning: How to Develop and Implement a Successful Strategy,* Bankers Publishing Company, Boston, 1985.

This information allows you to understand where you are today so that you can plan for tomorrow. In general, the plan should maximize your strengths, minimize or improve your weaknesses, take advantage of your opportunities, and eliminate threats to the bank so as to be a better financial intermediary in the years to come.

Analysis of the bank's SWOT should include your current financial condition and performance, economic and demographic conditions of the market in which you operate, customer and shareholder perceptions, competitive stance, as well as internal factors. Your competitiveness can be analyzed by examining your market position, structure, and power. Major threats facing the bank typically include local competitors and regulatory burden faced by all community banks. A market survey can be a useful tool in analyzing these factors. Internal factors can be brought to light through office and director survey questionnaires focusing on department management, communication and delegation issues, and other interdepartmental factors directly or indirectly affecting performance.

After you have completed all facets of the analysis of your current situation and determined the strengths and weaknesses of your organization, the future course of your financial institution must be envisioned by developing or revising your corporate mission. Once you know where you are headed—1, 3, 5, 10, and 20 years from now—then you can formulate goals and objectives for your institution. These goals and objectives are both financial and nonfinancial in nature and change in priority year after year as the bank is faced by internal changes and external contingencies.

We believe that the suitable strategic planning horizon is 3 years. External factors and regulatory changes impacting your financial institution are too great to determine long-term plans greater than 3 years. For example, in 1989 we saw

FIRREA, followed by the Bank Control Act of 1990 and FDICIA in 1991. In 1994, we had the Community Development Banking Act as well as the Reigle-Neal Interstate Banking Act. In 1996, we had the SAIF/BIF reconciliation bill. These significant federal banking legislative enactments make planning beyond 3 years almost impossible. Thus, your plan should be flexible. Further, by updating your plan each year—on a rolling 3-year basis—you can take into consideration the federal legislative impacts upon your financial institution.

It is crucial to develop realistic and pragmatic financial and nonfinancial goals and objectives. This book discusses this issue in detail and highlights the development of strategic action plans to implement the goals and objectives determined by the board and management. Strategic action plans are assigned to responsible officers and management members and are measured on an annual basis and can be utilized in the evaluation of management performance.

Finally, this book concentrates on what to do with your strategic plan once it has been developed. As noted earlier, don't set it aside. Review and revise the plan on an annual basis, and make decisions throughout the year based upon the goals and objectives of the strategic plan. A strategic planning retreat can provide senior management and the board with dedicated time toward working together as a team to review the previous strategic plan and to develop the revised strategic plan for the next 3 years.

SUMMARY

Strategic planning for community banks is the key for their survival over the next 10 to 20 years. However, strategic planning is not a guarantee or a magic elixir for success, but rather should be used to determine the future course of your bank. Without strategic planning, the future will determine the course of your bank.

The remainder of this book will outline the necessary steps in the strategic planning process, a timetable for such a program, and additional sources of information regarding strategic planning. In addition, the roles of the board of directors and management, both prior to and after the strategic planning process, will be analyzed. Finally, the interface between strategic planning and bank operations will be examined.

CHAPTER 2

Significant Issues Affecting Strategic Planning

The depository financial institution industry is consolidating. During the decades of the 1960s and the 1970s, the number of commercial banks, savings and loan associations, and credit unions was rising. However, in recent years the number of depository financial institutions has decreased significantly. As you develop your strategic plan you must recognize this trend. To survive as an autonomous financial intermediary, you will have to outperform many other institutions which decide to sell out, merge, consolidate, or even fail.

As a first step in examining the significant issues affecting strategic planning, we need to define the phrase *community bank or thrift*. This definition is actually quite simple—financial institutions (commercial banks and savings institutions) of less than $300 million in assets are generally perceived in the industry as community banks. We should probably start out by defining *community banking* vis-à-vis the entire banking industry. As of March 31, 1997, there were 8,363 commercial banks and 1,407 savings institutions that were under $300 million in size. These totals equal 88.49 percent of all commercial banks and 74.60 percent of all thrifts within the United States. Clearly, the community banking organizations in this country make up the lion's share of all depository financial intermediaries, regardless of what you read in *The Wall Street Journal* and/or the *American Banker*. The community bank is the local financial depository, and how it operates and grows and thrives within your community will directly affect the future of the entire community.

Why do we limit community banks to the $300 million asset size? The answer is that a commercial bank or savings institution of about $300 million in asset size will have gross revenues in the range of $25 million to $30 million and operating profits between $2 million and $3.5 million. These financial institutions are certainly not multibillion-dollar organizations, they do not operate in multiple states, they do not have international operations, and, in most cases, they are not highly diversified into 4(c)(8) nonbanking operations. Rather, in most cases, community banking organizations are "basic" banking operations which operate in suburban and rural communities throughout the United States.

COMMUNITY BANK CONSOLIDATION

Trends of consolidation are around us everywhere. In 1980, there were 14,435 commercial banks in the United States and 4,613 savings and loan associations. As of 1996, the number of commercial banks and savings and loan associations had declined to 9,528 and 1,334, respectively. At the same time, the total number of credit unions has fallen from 21,467 down to 11,392. As Table 2-1 highlights, the industry clearly is consolidating at an ever-more-rapid pace. In fact, the entire savings and loan industry is quickly

TABLE 2-1

Financial Institutions Industry

	1980	1990	1995	1996	1st qtr 1997
National and state banks & trusts	14,435	12,323	9,941	9,528	9,451
Savings banks	464	455	593	590	590
Savings & loans	4,613	2,992	1,436	1,334	1,296
Credit unions	21,467	14,505	11,887	11,392	

disappearing as a separate depository financial institution industry. With the recapitalization of the Savings Association Insurance Fund (SAIF) on September 29, 1996, and the speculation of a merger of the BIF (Bank Insurance Fund) and SAIF as of January 1, 1999, savings and loan associations seem to have a bleak future. Industry consolidation can also be examined by examining trends in the number of bank holding companies.

As of year-end 1996, there were 779 multibank commercial bank holding companies (Table 2-2) operating 2,905 banking subsidiaries (Table 2-3). At the same time, there were 4,350 one-bank holding companies. Adding the above numbers indicates that, in reality, there are only 5,129 commercial bank financial institution entities, not the 9,528 separate charters noted previously. These numbers would indicate that consolidation is therefore continuing at an even more rapid pace, and strategic planning is essential to compete and survive in the competitive, risky, uncertain banking environment.

What is driving this consolidation? Bank and savings and loan failures have been significant factors in the bank consolidations over the last decade and a half. The number of bank failures has been a rollercoaster, increasing from 16

TABLE 2-2

U.S. Banking Structure—Bank Holding Companies

	1988	1990	1995	1996
One-bank holding companies	4,854	4,817	4,406	4,350
Multibank holding companies	978	951	790	779
Total bank holding companies	**5,832**	**5,768**	**5,196**	**5,129**

TABLE 2-3

U.S. Banking Structure—Subsidiaries of Bank Holding Companies

	1988	1990	1995	1996
Subsidiaries of OBHCs	4,854	4,817	4,406	4,350
Subsidiaries of MBHCs	4,288	3,952	3,069	2,905
Total holding company subsidiaries	**9,142**	**8,769**	**7,475**	**7,255**

TABLE 2-4

Bank Failures

Year	Commercial Bank Failures	Year	Commercial Bank Failures
1980	16	1989	206
1981	32	1990	168
1982	42	1991	127
1983	48	1992	122
1984	79	1993	42
1985	120	1994	13
1986	138	1995	6
1987	184	1996	5
1988	200	1997 (1st qtr)	0

banks in 1980 to 206 banks in 1989, and then moving back to 5 banks in 1996 (Table 2-4). Thrift institution failures during the 1980s and 1990s resulted in significant losses and the bankruptcy of the Federal Savings and Loan Insurance Corporation (FSLIC). A total of 747 Resolution Trust Corp (RTC) savings and loan resolutions occurred from August 9, 1989, until the RTC sunset at December 31, 1995 (Table 2-5). Of this total, 501 savings and loan resolutions were through purchase and

TABLE 2-5

Savings & Loan Failures

Year	FSLIC Assistance Merger	Management Consignment Program	Failures	RTC Resolutions	Total Failures
1989	3	—	7	43	53
1990				315	315
1991				231	231
1992				64	64
1993				27	27
1994				63	63
1995				3	3
1996				1	1
1997 (1st qtr)					0

assumption agreements (mergers with other banks and/or thrifts), 158 resolutions were insured deposit transfers to other financial intermediaries which assumed the deposits only, and 88 resolutions were liquidations resulting from a lack of interest by potential bidding parties.

The major reason for these failures and the subsequent reduction in the number of failures is profitability. Both banks and savings and loans exhibited profitability weakness during the 1980s (Table 2-6). The saving and loan industry experienced years of disastrous profitability during the period 1987 to 1990, whereas bank profitability slumped markedly but was never negative. As a result, the number of savings and loans falling into the hands of the RTC for resolution increased dramatically during the period 1990 to 1995, and the industry never fully recovered. Commercial banks' profitability in contrast achieved historically high levels as savings and loan profitability was finally starting to recover.

Also significantly affecting the consolidation of the community banking industry during the last decade and a half was the merger and acquisition wave in the industry. Table 2-7 highlights the volume of mergers and acquisitions of commercial banks during the period 1981 to 1997 (first quarter), when more than 5,953 mergers were consummated. Thrift mergers were also prevalent over the period 1980 to 1996 and like banks, had a strong geographical preference. During the late 1980s and early 1990s, bank mergers were prevalent in the midwest. In the mid-1990s, southern institutions were hot prospects (Table 2-8).

Offsetting the number of mergers and failures has been the increasing number of new bank and thrift charters, especially over the period 1991 to 1996 (Table 2-9). New bank and thrift charters have followed the geographical failure trend—first in the Midwest, then in the South, and now just about across the country. Combined, the net effect of bank failures,

TABLE 2-6

Bank and Savings & Loan Profitability ($ billions)

Year	Commercial Banks	Savings & Loans	Year	Commercial Banks	Savings & Loans
1985	17.7	4.2	1991	18.6	1.1
1986	17.4	1.5	1992	32.2	2.9
1987	6.2	(5.8)	1993	43.4	2.3
1988	24.9	(11.1)	1994	44.7	4.3
1989	15.8	(19.2)	1995	48.8	3.4
1990	16.6	(13.1)	1996	52.4	4.8
			1997 (1st qtr)	14.5	2.4

TABLE 2-7

Bank Mergers & Acquisitions

Year	Number	Year	Number
1981	359	1990	213
1982	422	1991	178
1983	354	1992	301
1984	323	1993	327
1985	394	1994	562
1986	486	1995	529
1987	347	1996	554
1988	281	1997 (1st qtr)	66
1989	257		

mergers and acquisitions, and new charters has been consolidation of the industry.

LIBERALIZATION OF BANKING STRUCTURE

Structurally the most important change in the banking industry over the past decade and a half has been the significant liberalization of banking structure throughout the United States. Whereas we entered 1984 with no interstate banking (except for grandfathered western bank holding companies), by July 1, 1997, all 50 states have interstate banking laws. Now, we also have national interstate branching (except for the states of Texas and Montana, which opted out). Thus, for the first time in the history of the United States, we have true national banking and branching. This is expected to lead to banks with branches throughout the United States. By the turn of the century, we shall see common household bank and thrift names throughout all 50 states, the results of which

TABLE 2-8

Bank Mergers & Acquisitions by Geographic Region

	Midwest		South		West		Northeast	
Year	No.	%	No.	%	No.	%	No.	%
1986		50.8		31.6		7.4		10.2
1987		49.2		33.6		9.7		7.5
1988		62.4		22.2		8.8		6.6
1989		45.9		29.9		15.0		9.2
1990		54.0		27.2		14.6		4.2
1991	115	64.6	39	21.9	20	11.2	4	2.2
1992	135	44.9	115	38.2	28	9.3	23	7.6
1993	112	34.3	158	48.3	26	7.9	31	9.5
1994	175	31.1	250	44.5	58	10.3	79	14.1

TABLE 2-9

Domestic U.S. New Bank and Thrift Charters

	New Banks (BIF institutions)	New Thrifts (SAIF institutions)	Total
1990–1991	105	N/A	105
1991–1992	72	N/A	72
1992–1993	59	10	69
1993–1994	49	18	67
1994–1995	104	6	110
1995–1996	147	10	157
Total	536	44	580

will be significantly increased competition owing to diversification and greater survivability of the community bank. For the first time in banking history community banks will have to compete with New York, southeastern, midwestern, and western banking conglomerates as well as the bank down the street and the statewide bank holding company at the same time. In just slightly more than a decade, banking competition in the United States has gone from a posture of local competition to a posture of national competition. This new competitive posture will continue to fuel mergers and acquisitions and produce further consolidation within the industry, all of which will significantly affect the strategic plans of community banks within their local markets.

INTERNATIONAL BANKS

International banks have made significant inroads into the U.S. banking system over the past 25 years. As of year-end 1996, international banks operated in excess of 867 offices (banks, branches, agencies, representative offices) throughout the United States. Over 50 percent of these offices are located in the New York metropolitan market, with 20 percent in the San Francisco and Los Angeles markets and another 10 percent in the Chicago market. International banks now control more than 23 percent of all domestic IPC (individuals, partnerships, and corporations) deposits and currently provide 30 percent of all commercial loans made each year within the United States. International bank competition results in increased competitive pressures placed upon U.S. multibank holding companies within states which trickle down to more aggressive in-state, multibank operations in local markets.

FEDERAL LEGISLATION

All depository financial institutions have been significantly affected by recent federal banking legislation. By far the greatest impact was a result of the Financial Institution Recovery, Reform and Enforcement Act of 1989 (FIRREA). This legislation established the Resolution Trust Corporation for purposes of "saving" the savings and loan industry. By the time of its sunset on December 31, 1995, the RTC had spent approximately $150 billion of taxpayers' money.

In 1991, Congress passed the Federal Deposit Insurance Corporation Improvement Act (FDICIA), which, from a banker's perspective, permitted the FDIC to micromanage commercial banks and thrifts and increase funding for the bailout of the savings and loan industry. FDICIA permitted federal regulatory agencies to control management payrolls and directors' compensation and to limit business activities of banks and thrifts with CAMELS* ratings of 3, 4, or 5. These

* C=capital, A=assets, M=management, E=earnings, L=liquidity, S=sensitivity to market risk.

higher-risk institutions could not add new directors or install new management without approval of the appropriate federal regulatory agency. In addition, total compensation of management at these institutions was reviewed by federal regulatory officials. FDICIA also enforced consumer compliance and CRA legislation previously passed and eliminated some federal regulatory agency discretion in determining when commercial banks and thrifts could be failed. The discretionary handling of weak banks and thrifts was replaced by a mechanical incentive system which failed commercial banks and thrifts when capital adequacy dropped below 2 percent of assets. As a result of these pronouncements, FDICIA became an onerous regulatory burden to the bank and thrift industry.

Congress was not, however, finished. In 1994, Congress passed both the Community Development Banking Act (CDBA) and the Riegle-Neal Interstate Banking Act. The CDBA encouraged the development of community financial institutions designed to assist low- and moderate-income neighborhoods. However, with very few community banks receiving substantial funding, the impact of the Community Development Banking Act is still open to question. The impact of the Riegle-Neal bill, which permitted interstate branching by banks throughout the United States as of June 1, 1997, is, however, readily apparent. By year-end 1996, more than 45 states had adopted some form of interstate branching through purchase, reorganization of affiliates already owned within the states, or through the commencement of de novo branching activities within the states effective June 1, 1997. Only the states of Texas and Montana have opted out of interstate branching. Prior to the Riegle-Neal bill, all 50 states had some form of interstate banking legislation permitting either national interstate banking or some form of reciprocal banking. Thus, for the first time in the history of the United States, financial institutions can operate nationwide. It is quite conceivable that as we enter the new century we will have 10 to 20 banking institutions operating nationally or regionally providing banking services under the same name. The days of local banking will be gone, and the ability of community banks to survive will be significantly affected. Only through sound strategic planning will the community bank be able to compete successfully with the nationwide banking organizations, which will control 80 to 90 percent of the deposits throughout the United States.

In spite of these major reforms already enacted, Congress struck again on September 29, 1996. The Deposit Insurance Funds Act of 1996 (DIFA) passed on this date was ostensibly to solve underfunding of the Savings Association Insurance Fund (SAIF). Prior to the passage of this legislation, SAIF funding was only 43 cents per $1,000 of deposits insured. SAIF was required, however, to maintain annual premiums of $1.25 per $1000 of deposits. Thus, to accomplish full funding, the DIFA required insured SAIF financial institutions to pay a one-time 65.7 basis point assessment. Further, beginning in 1997, annual SAIF and BIF premiums would be used to begin to pay off the Financing Institution Corporation (FICO) bonds which were issued in 1989 in conjunction with the passage of FIRREA. Commercial banks' BIF premiums are established at approximately one-fifth of SAIF premiums over the period 1997 to 1999. After this period, premiums are projected to be roughly equal. The act also allowed for higher premiums for higher-risk institutions based on capital and management ratings. The end result of this legislation will be payment for a portion of the savings and loan bailout.

Note also that several provisions of this legislation have ominous future impacts upon savings and loans and other thrifts. Of particular pertinence is the potential for the merger of the BIF and SAIF funds on or about January 1, 1999. Prior to this occurring, however, Congress would need to pass legislation which for all intents and purposes would eliminate the federal savings and loan and federal savings bank charters, eliminate the Office of Thrift Supervision, and place control of these institutions under the Office of the Comptroller of the Currency. At the same time, the states would be under pressure to convert state federal savings and loans, mutual savings banks, and state savings banks into either state savings banks or state commercial banks to maintain parity. Thus, by the year 2000, there may not be a thrift industry whatsoever. An entire industry will have been eliminated through operation of law with only the commercial banking industry and the credit union industry remaining. The ramifications of these legislative acts will affect significantly your strategic planning. Increased competition and increased banking powers will require greater and more in-depth planning to ensure survival.

PROFITABILITY AND CAPITAL ADEQUACY

As noted earlier, profitability of the commercial banking industry reached historical levels over the period 1994 to 1996. This profitability has resulted in higher levels of retained earnings and capital at commercial banks and bank holding companies. The savings and loan industry has also benefited from recent profitability. At year-end 1990, the commercial banking industry had an average capital to total asset ratio of 6.46 percent. By March 1997, this average had increased to 8.47 percent.

From a planning perspective, this means that you should feel some hesitancy to assume a continuation of increased profitability and strong capital adequacy in your goals and objectives. This semi-doomsday approach is bolstered by strong signs of increasing consumer installment past due balances, charge-offs, and increased loan loss provisions. These factors indicate that the next 5 years may not be as profitable, and capital growth may level off. Your strategic plan will therefore need to ascertain what profitability and capital adequacy problems may occur and the best methods to react to those pressures into the future.

COMPLIANCE

The financial institutions industry has also been significantly affected by social reengineering by the federal government. This social reengineering started in 1977 when Congress passed the Community Reinvestment Act. Recent legislation discussed previously has also expanded adherence to consumer compliance and fair credit lending conditions, and as we begin the last third of the decade the emphasis on compliance will continue. Until the early-1990s safety and solvency issues were paramount. Now, however, most regulatory problems faced by commercial banks and thrifts are compliance-oriented, with a trend toward Community Reinvestment Act problems (i.e., discriminating against low- and moderate-income neighborhoods and minority groups), consumer compliance issues (i.e., discrimination against minority borrowers), or fair credit lending provisions. Compliance is of such importance that if you have an unsatisfactory compliance examination, do not even consider a merger or acquisition or even opening a de novo branch.

In recognition of this trend, as you develop your strategic plan, compliance issues should be a point of emphasis. Although federal legislation may be rolled back eventually, do not count on regulatory relief over the next several years. A posture of willing enforcement of compliance protocols will be well received by regulatory authorities in the near future.

PRODUCTS AND SERVICES

By far one of the most important aspects in the development of your strategic plan will be to establish the goal of implementing new products and services. In the past, many community banks have operated in a traditional manner and forgone opportunities to provide new products and services such as equipment leasing, life insurance, tax preparation, investment advisory, management advisory, mutual funds, courier services, and other 4(c)(8) activities noted on Table 2-10. By the year 2000, banks may also be able to provide full service real estate brokerage services and secondary mortgage market services. To a great extent, only staff capabilities are the limiting factor. If your institution thinks only in historical terms, you will not survive as a financial institution. New profitable products and services should be implemented, and existing, unprofitable products and services should be eliminated.

TECHNOLOGY

According to the trade publications, all depository financial institutions should now invest in technological improvements. However, technology is not a panacea to profitability or survivability. You should utilize or implement only technology that assists in providing better service to your customers and improving profitability. Rather, your strategic plan should examine available technological improvements on a cost-versus-benefit basis. Technology is but one vehicle for improving customer service at lower cost. You should not invest in technology simply because your competition has

TABLE 2-10

Selected 4(c)(8) Activity Alternatives

Selected 4(c)(8) Activity Alternatives
Mortgage banking
Consumer finance
Investment and financial advising
Personal or real property leasing
Bookkeeping and data processing services
Credit life, accident, and health insurance underwriting
Courier services
Sale of money orders, travelers' checks, and savings bonds
Discount securities brokerage
Tax preparation and planning
Collection agency services
Credit bureau services
Personal property appraisals
Check guaranty and vertification services
Appraisal, advising, and brokerage of commercial real estate properties
Community development advisory and related services

done so. You might also want to think about investing in technology by replacing obsolete in-house computer systems with outsourcing to a service processor. Furthermore, if you do not have the expertise internally to examine technology issues, hire someone to assist you in the analysis. You will not go out of business because you do not have imaging in your local rural market. You may go out of business, however, if you overspend and buy technology which does not have customer demand and does not bring you cost efficiencies.

ANTITRUST ISSUES

As you are developing your strategic plan for the years to come and assuming you anticipate bank or branch mergers and acquisitions, keep in mind that the antitrust laws of the United States have not been repealed. Before you decide to merge with the bank across the street, make sure you calculate your Herfindahl-Hirshman Index (HHI) analysis to determine whether the merger is procompetitive or anticompetitive. If the merger will be anticompetitive, your merger will be denied. Simply doing your antitrust homework in advance will avoid significant costs, indirect and direct, incurred from going forward with an anticompetitive acquisition.

SUMMARY

Each of the issues noted are important considerations in your strategic planning endeavors. Some of these issues will affect your planning directly, and others may simply be background issues in the implementation of your strategic action plans. However, neglect of these basic issues facing community banks and thrifts may result in a strategic plan that is inadequate to meet current and future challenges in the banking industry environment and may over time contribute to making your institution ineffective and noncompetitive.

CHAPTER 3

Who Is in Charge of Strategic Planning?

Modern management jargon often includes a variety of industry-specific buzz words. However, use of the phrase *strategic planning* can result in misunderstanding. One argument is that true strategic planning for financial institutions is unrealistic because of the unpredictability of financial events. With some justification, the contention is that without an accurate forecast of the business environment, any operating assumptions and derivative planning projects are not suitable to the ever-changing banking environment. Such protestations misinterpret the concept of strategic planning. Consequently, the content and application of strategic planning for community banks are often misunderstood.

WHAT STRATEGIC PLANNING IS NOT

Strategic planning does not structurally or functionally predict events associated with the bank and its short- and/or long-term management. Advocates of strategic planning meet their biggest challenge in bank managers or directors who are intimidated by unprecedented changes within the industry.

Strategic planning is not budgeting, financial forecasting, goal-setting, or marketing. The individual attributes of budgeting, financial forecasting, goal-setting, and marketing lack the connection of strategic design creation. These are fundamental management tasks that must be blended to create a more meaningful end product.

STRATEGIC PLANNING ATLAS

Strategic planning should be used as the road map for daily, monthly, and long-range decisionmaking. Many directions and turns can be taken along the way depending upon changes in destination, environmental conditions, competition, and alternative routes. The objective of a strategic plan is to utilize predefined operating assumptions to provide a realistic written guide for the future path of the financial institution in achieving its goals and objectives. In other words, the strategic plan maps out what is likely to occur as the result of specific choices or decisions. For example, if the strategic plan focuses around growth through acquisitions of banks or branches outside the primary service area, the original estimates would assume a variety of scenarios that consider the potential impact upon earnings, operating systems, and personnel issues. When executing that plan, the scenarios outlined indicate to management the likely consequences to the organization based on decisions made by management.

ARE WE THERE YET?

The purpose of the plan is to assist management with making prompt and informed decisions and to project the most reasonable impact those decisions will have upon the organization. The plan helps the organization to avoid decisions made in a vacuum with little regard to long-range results or to the advantages or disadvantages of alternative decision-making scenarios. The strategic planning document itself can serve as a funneling device to department managers and supervisors who, by necessity, should be developing individual operating plans to help achieve the goals of the overall plan. This funneling helps to ensure that all areas of the bank are pulling in one direction. Departmental plans and activities can contribute to the realization of strategic goals rather than extraneous schematics which by design keep employees busy, but not necessarily productive. A strategic plan also gives employees a definitive sense of organizational direction which can be more reassuring than unclear goals and objectives that create caution or indecision.

The strategic plan serves as a tool for management to evaluate the staff and for board members to assess senior management. At appropriately planned intervals, determining what has been accomplished, why, and by whom is much easier if the planning document spells out specific actions, time frames, and individual responsibilities. In that light, the plan also serves as a measure of the success and failure of the entire organization at the end of each planned interval (quarterly or yearly, as determined).

Of course the need for strategic planning is accentuated more than anything by the revolutionary scope of change within the community banking industry. Commercial banking has changed more in the last 20 years than ever before. The most significant element is the rapidity of change within the industry. Specifically, the life cycles of a variety of financial services and products offered by banking organizations have become shorter and shorter. One example is branch banking, which emerged after World War II during an era of exploding suburbs. Branch banking reached its peak in the

1970s and is now declining as the end of this century nears. This life cycle spanned approximately 50 years. By contrast, the 6-month fixed-rate, money market certificate of deposit (often referred to as the *Super T*) gained popularity in the mid-1970s and peaked in the mid-1980s. Money market investment accounts offered greater liquidity and flexibility and became a more desirable savings instrument.

As this book will discuss, changes in the financial services industry are attributable to such factors as the forces of deregulation, changes in competition, and the reduction in cost of deploying technology, to name a few. Operating in such an environment without a detailed plan of direction and of how the organization will attain long-range goals is suicidal. In the long run, such operation will short-change employees, shareholders, and the community in which the organization operates.

HOW TO BEGIN THE PLANNING PROCESS

The responsibility for drafting the strategic plan varies from organization to organization. In the community banking environment, the responsibility is guided by the chief executive officer with input from key staff members. Note that strategic planning is not an assignment delegated to the marketing department—which often then substitutes its own marketing plan for a strategic plan. Strategic planning also is not a project to be assumed by the board of directors. In many cases, board members do not possess intimate knowledge of the day-to-day function of the bank. Nor do they possess the scope of expertise to apply new and more sophisticated banking practices to the evolutionary needs of the bank. However, it is up to the board to assign responsibility and deadlines for getting the plan started, completed, edited, and revised.

Depending upon the size of the financial institution and its business mix, the planning team may consist of one to three officers. In banks with more intricate branch delivery systems or a more diversified customer base, a planning team of five or six individuals might be necessary. Banking institutions with several subsidiaries or affiliates might require as many as 15 individuals who are intimately involved in the strategic planning process.

As planning responsibilities evolve, the senior planning team will confine itself more to defining broad strategic goals and objectives. Delegation of formulating long-range operating plans that contribute to the attainment of strategic goals filters down to various department heads and managers of functional areas within the bank. The board of directors is responsible for monitoring the ongoing progress of planning efforts. The board serves as a check and balance to support or question the goals, objectives, strategies, and actions incorporated into the planning document.

If your community bank does not yet have a strategic plan, the format for initiating strategic planning is quite different: The initial strategic planning process begins with the board of directors and senior management. Even though the board does not have the day-to-day knowledge of banking, the board is responsible for the overall direction of the institution. To accomplish the proper focus, specific information gathering must take place. A consensus of opinions is revealed through the responses to a comprehensive questionnaire provided to directors and management. The questionnaire focuses on information regarding the association's image, the board of directors, executive management, management, the operation of key functional areas, financial goals, and expansion opportunities available.

The information provided by senior management and the board of directors is then summarized and used to provide the core content of a 1- or 2-day strategic planning seminar retreat. Many times the retreat format utilizes an outside, objective consultant to help develop a focus for the board which incorporates the financial and nonfinancial goals and objectives of the community bank or thrift. From that planning seminar, strategic action plans are determined and a strategic plan document is drafted. Upon ultimate approval by the board of directors, implementation can be delegated to senior management and further to junior management and staff.

In subsequent years, senior management and staff should become more integrally involved with the strategic plan, and the board of directors should take on a more supervisory role. The smaller the banking institution, the more involved the board must be.

OBSTACLES TO PLANNING

The role of senior management in community banking continues to change, expand, and become more challenging. However, the number-one reason strategic plans are not completed is because management "doesn't have time to get the job done." Time constraints are certainly legitimate defenses to the design and accomplishment of an elaborate plan. However, lack of time may be the rationale used by a management that does not understand how to put a plan together, how to delegate responsibility for putting a plan together, or how to develop a format for the written plan itself. Planning takes practice. The more familiar the task, the easier it is to accomplish! The process of strategic planning can vary depending on management style, the size of the institution, the degree of urgency, the amount of available data and staff to assist, and the overall familiarity and comfort with planning.

STEPS IN THE STRATEGIC PLANNING PROCESS

Although the planning formats may vary, the fundamental elements of strategic planning are fairly consistent—whether they involve a two-branch community bank or a twenty-affiliate superregional bank holding company. The most essential components include:

1. Completing a situation analysis
2. Drafting a corporate vision and mission statement
3. Determining organizational goals and objectives
4. Identifying strategies for attaining predetermined goals and objectives
5. Defining actions or steps to execute various strategies
6. Assigning individuals to carry out suggested action plans
7. Establishing deadlines for completion of various action plans
8. Monitoring, evaluating, and revising planning components

SITUATION ANALYSIS AND CORPORATE VISION AND MISSION

An important first step is to analyze the current situation of the community bank or thrift. If you do not know where you are today, how can you possibly plan for tomorrow? After outlining the situation analysis, a corporate vision and mission should be prepared which will assist the board of directors, senior management, and staff in determining the overall understanding (vision) of the institution. Subsequent development of a corporate mission can be used to reveal the institution's goals and purpose to shareholders (if applicable), creditors, customers, and the general public. Outlining the corporate vision and the separate corporate mission will be discussed in Chapter 9.

ESTABLISHING GOALS AND OBJECTIVES

Establishment of goals and objectives is also an essential component of the strategic planning process. Establishing attainable and meaningful actions requires confining goals and objectives to the broadest scope possible which have a priority readily accepted over other goals and objectives. In addition to limiting the goals and objectives to those which are accepted as the most significant, it is helpful when developing a written strategic plan to divide goals into basic categories. The categories will vary from plan to plan, again depending upon size, structure, business mix, and other variables in the institution and its market. A commonly accepted structure divides organizational goals and objectives into three categories:

1. Financial
2. Nonfinancial
3. Marketing

Goals and objectives that are not included in the strategic plan are often incorporated into departmental operating plans. Generally limited to 3 years, goals and objectives are assigned for each year of the planning horizon. Attempting to develop a plan beyond a 3-year horizon is more complex and can diminish the document's overall credibility. Each goal or category of goals, for each plan year, should have its own set of strategies and actions, target dates, and assignment of responsibility.

Financial goals and objectives outline for senior management and staff the desired goals for the financial performance of the institution. These goals and objectives are contingent upon the financial strengths and deficiencies of the organization and the planning direction. Most strategic plans include financial goals encompassing total assets, equity capital, equity capital ratios, net income, return on assets, return on equity, earnings per share, investment value per share, market share, and key expense targets. Targets for specific loan categories and deposit products and other financial objectives are best left for narrower departmental plans. Financial goals also include all the desired past-due, charge-off, nonaccrual, and ORE ratios as well as dividend payout rates, loan-to-deposit ratios, loan-to-asset ratios, and growth calculations (i.e., growth in assets, deposits, and loans).

Nonfinancial goals encompass other types of objectives to be achieved by the community bank. Some items might include: Should the computer be replaced? Should a service processor be utilized? Do we wish to merge with another bank, or do we want to start branches? Should we sell? The nonfinancial goals are not usually directly involved in the annual financial budgets but are longer-term projects designed to improve the performance of the community bank. For example, the retirement of current directors and their replacement becomes a significant nonfinancial issue. Management succession is critical to the survivability of an institution. The types of products and services rendered to the public may determine the level of competitiveness in years to come. Chapter 10 outlines the nonfinancial goals and objectives critical to overall performance. All goals and objectives, whether financial or nonfinancial, will decrease in number and specificity as you venture further into the planning horizon.

STRATEGIC ACTION PLAN DEVELOPMENT

At this point, key goals and objectives have been determined for the institution. The next step in the planning process is to identify strategies and develop action plans to attain or accomplish those goals and objectives.

Various methods may be used to accomplish this task. Each strategy or action plan will have its own set of pathways, constraints, costs, and implications. The strategic planning process ultimately is an attempt to specify those strategies and actions which are most relevant to the successful attainment of goals and objectives.

Begin with a specific target. If the bank's strategic planning goal is to make $500,000, strategies and actions are available to the bank to accomplish this goal. This could involve increasing service charges, increasing lending volume, decreasing deposit rates, or perhaps revising investment strategies. Each of these strategies has its own set of potential reverberations on other planning activities. The challenge is to whittle away those that are likely to be ineffective, unreasonable, or costly or otherwise conflict with other planning priorities and responsibilities.

MONITORING, CONTROLLING, AND REVISING THE STRATEGIC PLAN

The final step in the planning process is to establish control guidelines or a monitoring method to gauge the progress of planning activities. Initially, the plan should establish what areas should be monitored. Obviously, goals and objectives that require the most attention would be monitored on an ongoing basis. Secondary goals and objectives can be monitored by department heads and managers who have closer contact with activities related to those specific targets.

Perhaps the most overlooked aspect of strategic planning is that the process never ends. As circumstances within the bank or in the external environment continue to evolve or change, the planning document must be updated and revised to reflect new planning realities. Events such as changes in managerial responsibilities, promotions, executive departures, the failure of a local savings and loan, the closing of a holding company branch, or the establishment of a competitive branch facility all would have significant repercussions on planning priorities and activities. A recession, a plant closing, a new plant opening, or an unexpected and dramatic shift in interest rates also might significantly alter the planning process and content. These and other situations are justification for monitoring and rewriting the planning document on a semiannual, if not quarterly, basis.

The most important aspect of monitoring and controlling the strategic plan is to revise the written strategic plan on at least an annual basis to reflect the changes in the banking environment. Utilize the same board of directors and senior management team to analyze the deficiencies which occurred during the year and to implement new goals and objectives and strategic action plans.

A vital residual benefit of developing a written strategic plan is that it reinforces a level of responsibility and accountability often lacking in community banking organizations. Names and dates on planning documents inspire action and follow through. Such a level of accountability avoids the "I thought you were going to do it" syndrome.

PRESENTATION OF PLANNING DATA AND RESULTS

The culmination of planning activities is the preparation of financial tables and pro forma balance sheets and income statements. Implicit in any strategic planning effort is the assertion that planning priorities stipulated in writing will contribute to the enhanced financial performance of the organization. Whether the plan calls for hiring a new loan officer, introducing a new product, altering service charge schedules, or improving internal communications, all goals and objectives, strategies, and actions must contribute to enhancing financial performance and subsequent shareholder value. Some goals and objectives are more measurable than others, but all must be justified on the basis of their contribution toward the organization's financial success. Without financial accountability, the strategic planning document is diminished in its credibility and importance.

As planning goals, objectives, strategies and actions are revised, the board and management can gauge the impact of alternative scenarios and actions on a financial return basis. Judging whether one course of action is more lucrative and beneficial than another is contingent upon the level of confidence in planning methods, assumptions, and the validity and veracity of information originally incorporated into the plan. Therefore, revisions to the original strategic planning document should have as much credibility as the original projections, with all procedures and methodologies being equal.

SUMMARY

Strategic planning can be a dynamic and gratifying activity for bank executives and managers. Developing and designing your first plan can also be one of the most painstaking, frustrating, confusing, and threatening experiences involved in managing an organization.

In the past, bankers were not required to be effective planners in their environment of mandated activities, interest rate structures, or geographic constraints. However, as legislative and regulatory authorities reallocate decisionmaking and entrepreneurial functions to financial institutions, the necessity and scope of strategic planning becomes a more vital managerial function.

The extremes of risks and rewards are an integral segment of the financial services industry. Bank management will continually be challenged to discern substance from shadow, trend from fad, and opportunity from false hope. The ability of bankers to maneuver their institutions within the perils of the transformed financial services environment is enhanced if the organization's strategic plan is designed to facilitate short- and long-term decision making.

CHAPTER 4

Situation Analysis—Part One, Internal Analysis

Conducting the situation analysis portion of the strategic plan is a lot like training camp for a professional ball team. The coaching staff (board of directors and/or trustees) calls the team (managers and key staff) together for a practice session. Each "player" has an assigned position on the team, but the team works as a unit to win the game. Every team will have a few superstars that always seem to know where to throw the ball. Every team will have its share of players with great potential who simply need coaching in the right direction.

The coaching staff's job is to assess the available talent and develop strategic plays (actions) to keep the ball under control and win the game. Management's job is to regularly evaluate the performance (strengths, weaknesses, opportunities, and threats) of the team as a whole and each management member and officer to determine how their abilities can improve the organization. They must also be aware of and prepared for actions taken by the other team (competitors).

An effective and successful season (the yearly strategic plan) is the result of focused training and practice. The team uses its performance (the situation analysis) to improve its game until it triumphs over the competition.

Completing a comprehensive, diagnostic investigation of the organization's strengths, weaknesses, opportunities, and threats (SWOT analysis) is the most valuable component of the strategic planning process. Information gleaned and conclusions drawn from a situation analysis enable the bank to more fully identify its capabilities for attaining its strategic goals. The situation analysis empowers the community bank to design a strategic plan that identifies goals, objectives, strategies, and actions. The SWOT analysis maximizes the use of organizational strengths, which can augment or help eliminate strategies which are impeded by deficiencies (weaknesses).

Minimizing or even neglecting to complete a thorough SWOT analysis would be a serious planning error. Bank executives who exhibit a cavalier attitude toward the self-assessment process often fail in their attempts to ascertain and define a purposeful strategic direction.

However, ego is not the major reason that many banks avoid completing a comprehensive situation analysis prior to developing a strategic plan. More often than not, the fear of discovering unseemly aspects of their own organization dissuades many senior executives from embarking on a path of self-assessment. By definition and by its very nature, the situation analysis goes straight to the core and often exposes both the beauty marks and warts, sophistication and incompetence of an institution. Too often bankers look at airbrushed versions of reality thrust upon them by unsavory consultants, condescending competitors, or uninformed boards of directors. The situation analysis brings that touched-up picture into focus. The blemishes are exposed, and ultimately those imperfections must be acknowledged.

If properly performed, the situation analysis will examine each functional area of the bank. Members of the planning team (including department managers) can and should take an active role in the analysis as it will help increase their understanding of the bank and of the impact that their roles have in the successes and failures of the institution.

The situation analysis planning process is most beneficial and effective when prepared internally by senior management and appropriate supervisory personnel. Unfortunately, many executives and managers cannot retain objectivity when completing their own self-analysis or that of competing executives in functional areas. In some instances, a situation analysis may be the appropriate point in the planning program to utilize an outside consultant who is willing and able to provide an unbiased SWOT examination of the organization.

Prior to beginning the situation analysis, the following guidelines will help organize the process and get it completed in a timely and efficient manner:

1. *Keep the project manageable.* Although analyzing everything from personnel and products to paper clips and paint might be valuable, the nature of strategic planning implies the big picture. Once the organizationwide plan has been developed, detailed operational planning will be easier to structure and implement.

2. *Establish a timetable.* Decide on a date for completion of the situation analysis when the project is first undertaken. A thorough situation analysis usually can be completed within 30 days and should take no longer than 60 days. With this time constraint, specific timetables for each task associated with the situation analysis should be prepared with a notation of individual responsibility for each item. Vaguely ascribed time frames invite procrastination, and without timeliness, a situation analysis loses much of its credibility.

3. *Keep the situation analysis relevant.* Limit the study to information which suggests prompt, positive actions. Data with no bearing on a final decision do not need to be gathered and analyzed.

4. *Decide what and who should be analyzed.* No single format fits all banks. However, an unbiased analysis of strengths and weaknesses for each functional area of the bank and department managers is imperative.

5. *Design forms for gathering information in advance.* Department managers can prepare appropriate forms for their functional areas prior to the initiation of the information gathering process. Forms prepared in advance stimulate thought regarding the situation analysis tasks. Later, delegating routine tasks of gathering information will be easier if the forms provide some guidance to subordinates and staff who have the responsibility for assembling all the data. Forms also serve another extremely important function—they can limit or even eliminate distortions. Planning forms which delineate specific information requirements focus a manager's attention on salient issues versus self-serving data. The situation analysis often includes several distinctive subsections: The exact number of subsections will vary, depending upon size, market, competition, business mix, and other characteristics of the institution. However, many community banks divide their situation analysis profile into a managerial and organizational analysis, market analysis, and financial analysis—a format which replicates that of the final planning document.

This chapter examines the managerial and organizational, financial, and nonfinancial aspects of the community bank's strengths, weaknesses, opportunities, and threats in order to determine the current posture and strength of the institution.

MANAGERIAL AND ORGANIZATIONAL ANALYSIS

The first step in this component of the situation analysis is to review the organizational chart and job descriptions of the bank. If job descriptions are not available, it is important to complete them in order to evaluate performance, responsibility, and accountability of each employee. Many commercial banks do not have updated job descriptions nor do they maintain accurate organization charts that convey reporting responsibilities and the work flow from functional area to functional area, or from individual to individual. An organization chart reflects how communications (should) flow within the organization. Again, if the organization chart is not current, every attempt should be made to update the information as part of the strategic planning process.

Analysis of the organizational structure of a community bank often reveals managerial deficiencies and/or weaknesses such as incompetence of subordinates, managers operating in functional areas which do not meet their talents, and questions of management succession which may have been glossed over in previous years. Furthermore, the organizational structure that is depicted on paper may be quite different from the functional performance of the institution. Reviewing the organizational structure and the management orientation may provide insight into some functional and divisional problems that need to be remedied.

The next phase of the analysis is to develop a series of questions and guideline topics. Tables 4-1, 4-2, and 4-3 are typical of areas to be addressed by members of the board of directors, senior management, and selected staff members. These issues should be customized to elicit salient insights, goals, and objectives for all functional areas in the bank.

Issues covered in the questionnaires should examine management, operational effectiveness, and results gener-

TABLE 4-1

Strategic Planning Issues

Mission statement — *Provide detailed commentary on each issue*

Perception of bank's image
- Public
- Business community
- Shareholders

Board of directors
- Focus of board meetings
- General effectiveness in guiding bank's direction
- Ability to plan for the future
- Communication of goals and objectives
- Community involvement
- Business development activities

Management (direct supervisor)
- Management capabilities:
  - Technical skills
  - Communication skills—upward/downward
  - Management skills
  - Delegation skills
- Community involvement
- Business development activities
- Management succession planning
- Training/employee development
- Profitability orientation

Financial goals	1999	2000	2001
• Asset size projection	______	______	______
• Loan growth	______	______	______
• Portfolio focus	______	______	______
• Deposit growth	______	______	______
• ROA	______	______	______
• ROE	______	______	______
• Net interest margin	______	______	______
• Dividend distribution (%)	______	______	______

Expansion opportunities
- Branching
- Acquisition/merger
- Other

Overall perception
- Strengths
- Weaknesses
- Opportunities

TABLE 4-2

Functional Area Analysis

Management (president's assessment of department manager)

- Management capabilities:
  - Technical skills
  - Communication skills—upward/downward
  - Management skills
  - Delegation skills
- Community involvement
- Business development activities
- Management succession planning
- Training/employee development
- Profitability orientation

Effectiveness of the functional area

- Level of customer service
- Level of internal support

Effectiveness of communication of the functional area

- Written reports
- Oral reports
- Informal communication
- Communication to the right people
- Communication impediments
- Interpersonal relationships

Effectiveness of the organization of the functional area

- Proper staff level
- Efficiently organized
- Expertise of support; staff properly trained
- Recommended changes to improve

Ability of areas to plan for the future

- Growth potential of area
- Types of planning
- Expertise to plan or to problem solve

Areas' understanding of bank goals and objectives

- Participation in budgeting
- Participation in planning

Strengths of the functional area

Deficiencies of the functional area

TABLE 4-3

Functional Area Analysis

Management (self-assessment)
- Management capabilities
  - Technical skills
  - Communication skills—upward/downward
  - Management skills
  - Delegation skills
- Community involvement
- Business development activities
- Management succession planning
- Training/employee development
- Profitability orientation

Effectiveness of the functional area
- Level of customer service
- Level of internal support

Effectiveness of communication of the functional area
- Written reports
- Oral reports
- Informal communication
- Communication to the right people
- Communication impediments
- Interpersonal relationships

ated within the bank's individual functional areas. Evaluation of the communication and interaction with consumers, businesspeople, and shareholders is equally important during the situation analysis. Other key areas which should be analyzed include the board of directors, the effectiveness of marketing and advertising, overall leadership of senior management, committee structure of the bank and board, as well as areas which may not be formally designated as departments within the bank.

It would be misleading to expect that self-administration of the situation analysis questionnaires will result in an unbiased assessment. Therefore, you may wish to utilize an outside consulting group to promote confidentiality and to encourage full disclosure by executives and departmental managers. Interviews should also be conducted to probe for strengths and weaknesses prevalent throughout the organization. Consultants can minimize office politics and personal conflicts because their efforts remove the focus on personalities and/or individuals. Ensuring confidentiality allows each interviewee to disclose strengths and deficiencies of his or her own functional area and those of others in the institution. The overall strengths and weaknesses of the institution are developed from a consensus of questionnaire and interview comments.

As the interview consensus evolves, the apparent and latent strengths and deficiencies emerge and are identified in the final situation analysis report. Note that the efficiency or effectiveness of individual department heads, supervisors, and officers of the bank become by-products of the situation analysis process. Not only will individuals in charge respond to their own deficiencies (weaknesses) or strengths, they will offer their own insights regarding other department heads, senior managers, and perhaps even the board of directors.

The end product of the managerial and organizational analysis is a written report which identifies specific strengths and deficiencies (weaknesses) for each functional area and provides a specific list of recommendations which will capitalize on strengths or ameliorate deficiencies and/or weakness. These recommendations are integrated into the strategic planning document in the form of goals, objectives, strategies, or action plans.

FINANCIAL ANALYSIS

The financial analysis portion of the situation analysis process is completed in much the same manner as the managerial and organizational analysis. Usually the responsibility of the chief financial officer, the financial analysis lists financial strengths and deficiencies with brief explanations for such designations. Financial analysis should be based upon the past 5 years' financial history of the community bank. Comparisons of the bank's direction vis-à-vis the industry trends are important. Utilization of the Uniform Bank Performance Report (UBPR) or the Uniform Thrift Performance Report (UTPR) to compare the performance of the bank against its peers should also be stressed. Even if significant improvement within the bank is clear from the financial analysis, the bank still may be operating less capably than its peers. Peer-group comparisons are not panaceas, but they are worthy benchmarks to gauge the quality of the community bank and its performance trends. Other areas should be examined in addition to the UBPR and the UTPR, including industry statistics as published by Sheshunoff Information Services, SNL Securities, and other private corporations, as well as statistics compiled and distributed by the Federal Deposit Insurance Corporation, the Office of Thrift Supervision, the Office of the Comptroller of the Currency, the Federal Reserve System, and the Federal Financial Institution Examination Council (FFIEC). All of these sources should be reviewed to determine the financial strengths and weaknesses of the community bank. Also, do not forget the Federal Reserve's Functional Cost Analysis which *may* be applicable to your particular institution, especially if there is a functional cost program within the institution. This program is still underachieving its potential throughout the industry but can be worthwhile as an analytical tool in determining strengths and weaknesses and efficiency from a financial perspective.

Significant financial analysis issues might include the following: loan demand, overhead expense, loan losses, earning assets, loan and deposit growth, asset/liability/

GAP management, deposit composition, capital formation, net interest margins, fee income, investment performance, overall profitability, ROA, ROE, salary and bonus expense, investment value, stock trading activity, dividends, dividend growth, loan loss reserves, other real estate owned, and new accounts. To a great extent, each of these factors is examined in the stock valuation. The stock valuation will provide key insights into financial analysis issues and serve as a basis for determining financial objectives included in the final strategic planning document (see Chapter 6 on valuation).

Written exposure of deficiencies and weaknesses can be uncomfortable. After the initial shock, the planning process should be able to proceed more quickly, smoothly, and positively. If management and staff will understand and accept the benefits that can be gained from completing a situation analysis, a positive atmosphere of anticipation and change can stimulate the acceptance of challenges and planning for the bank's future success.

SIGNIFICANT ISSUES (HOT TOPICS)

At this point in the situation analysis, significant issues affecting the community bank or thrift should be clearly defined. Every organization accumulates excess baggage. It is imperative that these areas be addressed candidly and honestly to accurately determine the strengths and weaknesses of the organization and to take advantage of opportunities. For example, does it make good business sense to retain an incompetent employee, even if he or she is a relative of the president? Are there older members of the board who do not and have not actively participated for a number of years?

Spend some time in the situation analysis examining the significant issues ("hot topics") that face your financial institution. This is an area where an outside consultant can be of tremendous assistance. Revealing sensitive issues and discussing them with the board and senior management can be done in such a fashion that it eliminates personal conflicts and concentrates on how these topics adversely affect the financial institution.

Hot topics discussed during the situation analysis will thread their way back through the goals and objectives outlined by the analysis. They will again be stressed during the strategic action plans to eliminate them as significant issues and to work them into the overall improvement of the financial institution. Avoiding the significant issues faced by the institution would be a critical mistake in the strategic planning process.

NONFINANCIAL ANALYSIS

The final portion of the internal situation analysis is what we have termed the *nonfinancial analysis,* or the kinds of issues which obviously have financial ramifications but are nonfinancial in nature. The following list is typical of areas that could and should be discussed and analyzed in the nonfinancial analysis:

- The issue of continuing as an independent financial institution or deciding to sell
- The issue of merging with another institution or acquiring other banks, thrifts or their branches
- De novo branch expansion
- Examining new products and services
- Improving the marketing and sales culture
- Improving the training of employees
- Management education
- Board of director education
- New computer systems—either internal or outsourced

- New physical facilities, including new main office building, operations center, and so on
- New employees based upon new functions (i.e., new products and services)
- Formation of a bank or thrift holding company
- Nonbanking activities approved for thrifts and banks and their holding companies
- Alternative delivery systems
- Degree of technological improvement of services
- Effect of competition
- Regulatory burden

This list is not exhaustive. A more detailed discussion of nonfinancial goals and objectives is presented in Chapter 10. Each community bank has a different set of priorities and is a different business. Consequently, some of these issues may or may not be germane to your organization. Each issue must be analyzed on its own merits as to its strengths, weaknesses, opportunities, and threats and given the same consideration as any of the financial aspects. Not all aspects of the financial institution's future will be financial in nature, and thus nonfinancial aspects should also be a part of the strategic plan for the next 3 years.

SUMMARY

In almost every planning instance, the situation analysis can be the most challenging component to complete. Although glossing over the unpleasant deficiencies or weaknesses discovered during the process may be tempting, a thorough, unbiased assessment will generally confirm many attributes as well as negative aspects which management has already acknowledged or suspected.

Successful completion of the situation analysis is essential for a comprehensive and useful strategic planning document. Objectivity in gathering and evaluating data ensures accuracy and veracity of the plan. The comprehensive situation analysis encompasses a stock valuation, management and organizational assessments, and a detailed examination of financial performance results and expectations. Moreover, the timeliness of data along with participation by a broad cross-section of employees during the process contributes greatly to formulating conclusions and recommendations which become the basis for establishing broad planning goals and objectives.

CHAPTER 5

Situation Analysis—Part Two, External Analysis

In Chapter 4 we examined the internal aspects of the situation analysis. However, community banking organizations are affected by external factors as well as internal factors. Thus, an important part of the situation analysis is an examination of the external parameters affecting the future condition and performance of the community bank. This chapter will emphasize regulatory burdens, competition between community banking organizations and among financial service corporations, technological delivery services, marketing research surveys and marketing culture, and, finally, external, exogenous, demographic, financial, and economic information which affects the marketplace served by the community bank. Each of these factors must be analyzed for their strengths, weaknesses, opportunities, and threats vis-à-vis the community bank within its market place. Regardless of how well the bank improves itself internally, if it cannot effectively compete within the marketplace, its potential is limited. Thus, a careful assessment of the external forces which impact the survivability of the community bank is essential in determining the future course for the financial institution.

In addition to an ever increasing number of competitors who provide the same or similar services as community-based commercial banks, other competitors provide different and more desirable services. This has significantly hampered the growth and vitality of community banks. The emergence of nontraditional competitors, such as brokerage companies and retailers, has made it possible to package routine banking services with more exotic investment services, insurance products, and financial planning assistance. Many of these services are difficult or even illegal to offer through the traditional community bank delivery system.

AUTOMATIC TELLER MACHINES (ATMS), POINT OF SALE TERMINALS (POS), HOME BANKING, AND ACCOUNT IMAGING

The relentless introduction of new and improved technological advances continues to permeate the front lines of community banking. However, marketing prerequisites are not in the development of technology but rather in strategic positioning to retain and capture market shares.

Technology enables marketing professionals to become even more efficient and effective. Today's most valuable progress in technology may be in capturing, storing, replicating and accessing data which relate to individual banking habits, productivity, and profitability. As financial institutions gather additional information regarding customer usage patterns, more effective targeting of consumers whose banking habits indicate a greater likelihood for purchasing specific banking services and products is possible.

Operating efficiencies and marketing strategies have been and will continue to be significantly affected by deployment of new banking technology. As technology adapts to specific product formats, banks will market value—added services to customers as evidenced through the evolution of the basic checking account. As the result of debit cards, ATMs, payments by phone, and overdraft credit features, today's checking account is more valuable. As the cost of deploying technology diminishes, financial institutions can reduce the cost of operational and product delivery expenses associated with such enhancements through improved check processing, computerized teller terminals, and lower-priced ATMs. Moreover, technological innovations may provide community banks with an opportunity to reallocate personnel expenditures to more productive endeavors, such as direct sales.

Determining the current status of a community bank should include a comparison of the technology available within the marketplace as well as the technology utilized by competitors. However, if an institution utilizes every new technological improvement, the costs could be considerable. Before offering a modern delivery system to customers, the bank and / or thrift should determine their ability (including internal skills and sufficient staffing) to provide a more efficient system. Obviously, one of the most important improvements and opportunities available to community banks over the next decade will be technologically delivered services which allow community-oriented institutions to compete with state and nationwide bank holding companies and thrifts.

REGULATORY BURDEN AND STRATEGIC PLANNING

One of the most uncertain areas to predict is the impact of federal legislation and regulation on strategic planning. It is extremely difficult for community banks and thrifts to plan for future performance when there is no way to determine what the playing field will be 2 to 3 years into the future. As strategic planning evolved, it was customary to consider a strategic planning horizon of 10 years. The time frame was later tightened to include 3 to 5 years. The latest approach—this book—emphasizes 3 years as the limit for how far the plan should project. The most important rationalization for this myopia is the impact of federal legislation and regulatory burdens placed upon community banks and thrifts.

The current wave of rapid regulatory change is really not much different from what happened back in the late 1970s and early 1980s. At that time, banks and thrifts were permitted to market IRA accounts. Then, along came Congress and completely abolished the flexible personal IRA. Today, when planning 3 years into the future, it is of no small concern that 2 years out, the industry may drastically change. For example, the Deposit Insurance Funds Act, enacted in September 1996, implied that the BIF and the SAIF will be merged by January 1, 1999. The passing of this bill has tremendous implications for the future of federal savings and loans and federal savings banks. As we know them today, there may not be any SAIF institutions remaining by the turn of the century. How can community banks and thrifts forecast their future when by operational law they may disappear in the corporate structure in which they now operate? The resultant organization may be competitively different from the banks and thrifts of today. Such restructuring possibilities should encourage a more focused strategic planning approach to ensure the survival of the financial institution into the twenty-first century.

In the past decade, community banks and thrifts have dealt with such legislation as the Competitive Equality Banking Act of 1987 (CEBA), the Financial Institutions Reform, Recovery, and Enforcement Act in 1989 (FIRREA), the Federal Deposit Insurance Corporation Improvement Act of 1991 (FDICIA) , the Community Development Banking Act of 1994 (CDBA), and the Riegle-Neal Interstate Banking Act of 1994. These major federal legislative enactments as well as over 100 new rules and regulations have changed the administrative and operational landscape for community banks and thrifts and forced extreme compliance measures on all banks and thrifts. Thus, focused prioritization in planning has become increasingly more meaningful than simply increasing lending and depository services. Internal auditing, consumer compliance, fair credit lending, equal credit administration, equal credit opportunity employment, and the Community Reinvestment Act are critical areas of concern in today's banking environment.

MARKET RESEARCH, MARKET SURVEYS, AND MARKET ANALYSIS

The viewpoint on how well a bank is doing is biased when taken from the perspective of the board of directors, management, and staff of the institution itself. The viewpoint of an outside, independent survey can best determine how the institution is perceived by the community and how it is performing. A valuable instrument for strategic planning is market research to identify the types of services and products desired by consumers and what customers and the community think of existing products and services. An external survey is not necessary every year, but about once every 3 years you should investigate how well the bank or thrift is doing in the community from the viewpoint of others outside the institution. In addition, provision of new products and services as well as the retention of current services should be based not only on what you think the customers want but also on market research of what customers and potential customers indicate they want. This type of market research and market survey analysis is necessary for a community bank and/or thrift to understand its strengths, weaknesses, and opportunities throughout the marketplace over time.

Larger community banks have an internal marketing staff that accomplishes a considerable amount of market research as well as market surveying. Smaller community banks must hire outside professional marketing research and survey firms to assist them. In both cases, market research and market surveying should be considered a part of the overall marketing budget and should not be discounted or eliminated. Unfortunately, short-term results may not seem as effective as spending another $50,000 in advertising.

The purpose of a market survey is to check the conformity of management's understanding of the community bank with perceptions of the community. Management may consider the institution to be a blue-collar, middle-class community bank. The surveys could reveal that it is perceived as a white-collar, upper echelon bank. This would be a real shock! As a part of the strategic planning analysis, external market research and surveying is a valuable tool in determining how well the bank or thrift is doing, how well it is perceived, and what would make it a better community bank within the community.

Market analysis encompasses more than market research and market surveys. The following sections will discuss the need to analyze external impacts upon the banking institution such as population growth, household formation, median family income, per capita income, and the like. Analysis of external forces will assist in determining what effect competitive, economic, demographic, and financial pressures have on the financial condition and performance of the institution and how to relieve those pressures through improved performance. A comprehensive strategic plan reflects both internal and external influences in which a financial institution operates. Failure to analyze outside forces could adversely affect the results of the strategic planning process and create unattainable objectives.

DEMOGRAPHIC, ECONOMIC, AND FINANCIAL STATISTICS

Analysis of the demographics, economics, and financial statistics of a particular market can determine the trend as well as the rapidity of growth, or alternatively the secular stagnation or decline of the market. For example, household formation types and trends, economic income levels of the population, the current status of industrial development, and community job trends are all significant factors which affect the growth of the institution, improvement in profitability, and the status of a banking institution within the market place. To develop appropriate financial and nonfinancial goals and objectives, it is necessary to understand external market trends in the market, its growth, and its quality.

Table 5-1 outlines various economic, demographic, and financial statistics to analyze to determine the impact of external factors upon the strategic plan. Each banking market is different, and thus some information may be readily available in a major metropolitan or suburban market and yet relatively inaccessible or far more aggregate in nature for a rural county market. Regardless of the depth of information, advantages may be gained by examining the economic and demographic data to determine appropriate strategic planning for the growth of your community bank.

COMPETITIVE ANALYSIS

The final aspect of external market analysis is by no means the least important. Analyzing the strengths and weaknesses of a financial institution is not complete without comparing the financial condition and performance of one financial institution vis-à-vis others within the market. Thus, it is necessary to ascertain competitors within the "banking market." Most banking markets are defined by

TABLE 5-1

Economic and Demographic Statistics to Be Analyzed

- Population trends
- Age categories of population within banking market
- Household formation
- Breakdown by category of households by age, marital status, and number of individuals per household
- Average income per household
- Median income per household
- Per capita income per household
- Per capita income per individual
- Median income per individual
- Retail sales within the market
- Manufacturing statistics
- Number of new business starts
- Personal bankruptcies
- Business bankruptcies and failures

the Federal Reserve. If they have not been defined, the market area can be approximated using a single county or portions of several counties if the bank or thrift is located in the corner of a county.

Concentration should be on growth of bank and thrift assets, deposits, loans, and capital vis-à-vis competitors within the banking market. Is the institution growing faster or slower? Is growth stagnant while others are moving forward? The stronger the institution, the better will be its growth in basic asset and liability ratios. However, comparisons should also be made in terms of income statement ratios such as rate of return on average assets and rate of return on equity, as well as rate of growth in capital in contrast to peer groups.

Financial institution comparisons including call reports and statement of income earnings and dividends can be obtained from the FDIC, FFIEC, or from private sources such as Sheshunoff Information Services. Call reports not only provide the necessary information to analyze gross numbers (such as growth in assets, size of deposits) but also are so detailed that they allow scrutiny of changes in consumer installment loans, the amount of commercial loans, or the efficiency ratios and noninterest expense accounts. On a regular basis, your bank or thrift should examine its performance within the banking market in comparison to its competitors.

One can determine how viable a particular banking market is by examining ratios such as population per bank, population per banking office, deposits per bank, deposits per banking office, per capita income, and the like. Comparing population, housing, and income data can help determine the viability and growth of your banking market and those markets in which you plan to merge or branch.

Finally, the competitive posture within the banking market can be analyzed by determining the degree to which mergers can take place between institutions. The statistical technique known as the Herfindahl-Hirschman Index (HHI) as outlined by the Department of Justice Merger Guidelines of 1982 (as amended), can determine which financial institutions within a specific banking market can be merged while maintaining competition in the market. The HHI can determine whether a banking market is unconcentrated, moderately concentrated, or highly concentrated. Mergers that lessen competition can be challenged by the Department of Justice under U.S. antitrust laws. Remember, if you are going to affiliate or merge with an institution in a different banking market, the HHI analysis is not necessary because the merger will not change or adversely impact competition within that marketplace. However, if the banking market is not analyzed to determine which institutions would be best suited for affiliation, you deal at your own peril.

At least annually, run the HHI analysis to redetermine within your banking market which institutions are eligible for affiliation. As other banks and thrifts merge within the market area, or statewide or national banks and thrifts enter the banking market, the HHI will change. Opportunities not available last year may become available this year.

SUMMARY

The situation analysis cannot be limited to only an internal analysis of the financial institution. Each institution's performance must be correlated to exterior factors, such as technology, regulation, demographic trends, and competition within the market. Market research is but one method to determine the reputation and credibility of your institution, the demands for various products and services, and the degree of acceptance of current products and services in the market. All this analysis should be part of the external analysis of the situation analysis to determine overall strengths, weaknesses, opportunities, and threats of the community banking institution. Combined with the internal analysis, the complete situation analysis provides your financial institution with a fact pattern necessary to establish reasonable goals and objectives and action plans to meet those objectives.

CHAPTER 6

Valuation

For practical business reasons, measuring the change in a financial organization's stock price is essential to determine strategic planning performance. However, many community-oriented financial institutions do not have a strong market or do not trade in sufficient quantities to permit market valuations which reflect the intrinsic value of their securities. Thus, performing a stock valuation is essential. Determining the value of the financial institution's stock prior to initiating strategic planning will assist in assessing the overall performance of the institution. Since some community thrifts are still mutual rather than stock organizations, per-share security valuations are not possible. However, aggregate valuations of the mutual thrift organizations are possible, and the techniques utilized in this chapter for determining overall aggregate value and its change over time are just as applicable as if we were measuring the value of stock of commercial banks and stock thrifts.

Under appropriate circumstances, market values may reflect the "fair market value" or "fair value" of the securities of a bank or thrift holding company. However, under the conditions faced today, community banks and thrifts often do not have a true market value, and financial analysis must be undertaken to determine value. Profiled briefly below are several valuation techniques utilized in stock valuations.

DISCOUNTED CASH FLOW–INVESTMENT VALUE

The discounted future cash flow technique is based on the principle that the worth of a business is equal to the net present value of future net cash flows. The most valuable element of the valuation is the forecast of future available cash flows. Deriving these figures requires a projection of the balance sheet and income statement of the organization being valued.

ADJUSTED BOOK VALUE TECHNIQUE

Future cash flows of a community bank or thrift are not known with certainty. Thus, the adjusted book value technique provides an alternative approach to valuing the institution. This technique involves a determination of the fair value as a going concern of all assets and liabilities of the bank, including intangible assets.

MARKET COMPARABLE APPROACHES

Two market comparable approaches may be considered: (1) price (market value)–earnings multiple and (2) price (market value)–book value ratio. The price-to-earnings multiple (P/E) involves six steps:

1. Analyze the economic environment.
2. Conduct an in-depth analysis of the banking industry.
3. Analyze the subject organization, which includes a comprehensive analysis of the financial institution's competitive and financial position.
4. Select a set of similar or comparable publicly traded or recently acquired banks or thrifts. Note that many community banks are considerably smaller in terms of assets than comparable publicly traded peers, and in those cases this market approach would not be appropriate.
5. If comparable publicly traded banks or thrifts are identified, identify the similarities and differences in asset quality, deposit mix, financial performance, and so on and make adjustments to put the banks or thrifts on a comparable basis.
6. The final step involves multiplying the appropriate P/E multiple by the most recent 12-month earnings or earnings-per-share figure of the institution being valued. The earnings period of the appropriate comparable banks' P/E multiple should match, with as close proximity as possible, the earnings period of the bank/thrift being valued.

The second market comparable approach is the market price–book value ratio. This concept is similar to the P/E multiple except that the average market price–book value ratio of comparable banks or thrifts is multiplied by the book value of the organization under analysis. As with the P/E multiple analysis, similar problems arise in finding true market comparable institutions. Further, unadjusted book value represents an accounting and tax concept only, and therefore the book value may or may not have any relationship to fair value of the bank or thrift.

CAPITALIZATION OF DIVIDENDS

In this approach, dividend yields of comparable publicly traded institutions are compared with the historical dividends paid by the subject institution. For example, if comparable publicly traded institutions were found to have an average dividend yield of 5 percent whereas the subject company paid a dividend of $0.50 per share, then the implied per share value would be $10.00 ($0.50 / 0.05). This approach is used more often in conjunction with minority interest than with controlling interest.

In a valuation of a controlling interest, the dividend paying capacity is more important than the historical dividends paid owing to the ability of the controlling interest to dictate future dividend policy. Dividend capacity is the amount of earnings available net of earnings required to maintain adequate capital levels. Dividend capacity could also be used as an indication of the cash flow provided by the institution.

MARKET PRICE

In theory, market price reflects the true value of any underlying security. This assumes that the trading volume of the security is sufficient to provide a liquid market for small to moderate blocks of stock to be traded by willing buyers and sellers in an arms-length transaction. Typically, the market for the common stock of a community banking organization would not meet these standards necessary to establish fair market value. Therefore, historical trading prices at community banks are not directly utilized to determine fair market value.

PURPOSES OF STOCK VALUATIONS

In addition to utilizing the stock valuation for determining the success or failure of the implementation of changes resulting from established strategic planning goals and objectives, a valuation can also be used as a base for determination of incentive compensation, stock options, and other bonuses for senior management. A stock valuation is also critical in determining the price to pay for a merger or acquisition or the financial value of a branch, to establish a value for ESOP (or ESOT) redemption, to institute a value for corporate stock redemption, and ultimately to determine the worth of the financial institution should you decide to sell.

INCENTIVE COMPENSATION, STOCK OPTIONS, AND OTHER BONUSES

One of the most underused purposes of an annual stock valuation is as a base for determining executive performance. Executive compensation tied to stock price improvement is an interdependent measurement factor which incorporates financial and nonfinancial performance. Failure to maximize performance of *all* aspects of the institution negatively impacts the short-term and/or long-term stock price performance and, thus, executive compensation. Further, improvements in stock price directly achieves the goal of the board—to maximize shareholder value.

MERGERS AND ACQUISITIONS

Stock valuations are critical in mergers and acquisitions. If the acquisition has not been solicited, a different and less detailed valuation is prepared. In this case, the quarterly call reports, statements of income and dividends, and the Uniform Bank (or Thrift) Performance report (UBPR or UTPR) is obtained through sources such as the federal regulatory agencies (including via internet access) or private companies selling such information. This information should provide suitable figures for establishing an estimated valuation of the banking institution, which can then be augmented through due diligence prior to signing a formal agreement. Stock valuations are also used to determine the exchange ratio for consolidating organizations. In these combinations, the valuation process becomes political as well as financial and an independent valuation is essential. It is certainly not advisable to make a formal bid for another bank, thrift, branch, or other institution without an independent and impartial valuation.

PURCHASING AND SELLING BRANCHES

Throughout the nation, multistate bank and thrift holding companies are realigning their banking structures to concentrate on major markets and divesting rural and suburban branches. As a result, a number of bank and thrift branches are becoming available to community banks and thrifts. Weaker financial institutions are also selling off branches to enhance the appearance of their own financial statements. How do you take advantage of these opportunities? Your first action is a valuation.

Different valuation techniques are utilized for determining pricing for community bank and thrift branches.

When purchasing a branch, essentially the buyer pays a premium for the deposits of the branch and acquires for book value (or a negotiated price) the fixed assets of the branch. In many situations, the selling institution will not sell loans, unless they are specialized loans, such as agricultural or commercial loans, tied to the location.

Since the days of RTC failed savings and loan branches are long gone, it is not unusual for the premiums on deposits to run in the range of 8 to 10 percent. A recent trend toward the packaging of a regional group of branches is also underway. Selling institutions have seen that the costs associated with divesting a single branch are approximately the same for larger groups of branches. As a result, some smaller community banks are not having the opportunity to bid on grouped branch transactions. Successful community banks take a proactive approach to valuing a target and approaching a competitor to solicit the purchase of desired branches prior to announced divestitures.

ESOPS AND ESOTS

Some organizations utilize an ESOP or an ESOT for purposes of achieving employee ownership. Trustees of the ESOP or ESOT who purchase either authorized but unissued capital stock or redeem stock from the market place, should use a stock valuation conducted by an impartial, third party. An outside valuation will relieve the trustees of liability from disgruntled employees who believe that the stock has been purchased at a price significantly higher than its true value, thus reducing employee retirement benefits. The ESOP/ESOT valuation establishes an appropriate fair price and eliminates or mitigates liability of the trustees. The ESOP/ESOT valuation may also be used for corporate stock redemption by the holding company.

CORPORATE STOCK REDEMPTION

In most states, community banks are not permitted to repurchase their shares. Bank holding companies are able to do so as long as they are rated a CAMELS 1 or 2 and have no administrative problems. The holding company only needs permission from the Federal Reserve if the bank is not well capitalized. However, notice to the regulatory agencies is still recommended.

The redemption of corporate stock is the most common use of the holding company structure. In 1987 (current statistics are not available), more than 46 percent of all midwestern community one-bank holding companies redeemed stock within the first five years of their existence. Stock redemptions assist in increasing the liquidity and marketability of holding company stock, managing the shareholder base (through redemption of out-of-market or hostile shares), and eliminating excess costs associated with small shareholdings.

An independent valuation of the holding company stock is essential. If a stock redemption price is determined by the board of directors or management of the holding company, the institution risks being sued by disgruntled shareholders for wasting corporate assets by overpaying or underpaying and thus reducing shareholder values for redeemed shares.

Once established, a stock redemption policy made known to all shareholders will allow the board to redeem holding company stock on a regular or as-needed basis. Redemptions can be funded through earnings, use of capital, or, in the event of a major shareholder's death, through borrowings.

The corporate stock redemption program should be overseen by an outside consultant assisting the board of directors. Redemption practices themselves should be closely monitored. The bank holding company attempting to buy or sell stock may unintentionally violate "blue sky" laws, or worse, security regulations if handled incorrectly. A number of community banks and thrifts today have a redemption valuation performed on a quarterly basis. Since there is rarely a true market price for community bank or thrift securities, this valuation allows the holding company to establish a "price" to its shareholders. Shareholders can then more easily utilize their securities as collateral.

SELLING THE COMMUNITY BANK OR THRIFT

It is a fact that over the next decade, a number of banking organizations will be sold. Shareholders will desire to sell their stock, competition will become stronger, and the management of many financial institutions will be unable to cope with the pressures of survival. Whereas some may say that selling out is poor banking strategy, the sale of the bank is one way to realize shareholder value in a more liquid form than in community bank stock.

Assuming that an organization has reached the decision to sell through competent strategic planning, the stock valuation is utilized to determine value prior to putting the institution on the market. A valuation is essential to eliminating the risk of underpricing or overpricing the institution. To maximize shareholder wealth from this one-time sale, the stock valuation provides a minimum financial fair value. If offers come in under the minimum fair value price, simply reject those offers. Offers received at or above the minimum value require rational review by the directors and officers to reach a reasonable business judgment decision.

Hopefully, your banking institution will be sold only once. If you have no idea of the value of the institution, you will encounter significant problems trying to negotiate with an experienced bidding organization. Thus, a valuation is the key to success.

SUMMARY

A stock valuation is an integral component of the strategic planning process. A valuation allows the community bank or bank or thrift holding company to establish the framework for gauging financial performance and management competency. The valuation allows the holding company to determine incentive compensation or bonus payments. In addition, a stock valuation permits for corporate stock redemption, ESOP and ESOT stock purchases, and determination of the value of potential merger and acquisition bank and branch targets. Finally, a valuation establishes the minimum financial value in the sale of the bank. Regardless of the purpose, stock valuations provide critical information for key decisions.

CHAPTER 7

Selecting a Strategic Planner

A strategic plan will not write itself. We recommend utilizing the services of a professional planner for the initial strategic plan and thereafter on a periodic basis. Past experience indicates that an objective perspective produces a strategic plan that incorporates all facets, including contentious issues that may not be addressed by inside management. This chapter will address such areas as determining whether to use an external or internal planning team; how to select a strategic planning group; how to keep strategic planning efforts focused to ensure the development of a quality plan in a timely manner; and finally, the importance of the strategic planning retreat as a tool to assist with annual revisions and improvements to the strategic plan.

ADVANTAGES OF UTILIZING AN EXTERNAL STRATEGIC PLANNING FIRM

There is no shortage of strategic planners. They come in plain vanilla or the exotic variety. You can hire a one-person show or an entire team. The choice is yours. The first step is to select a strategic planner. Choosing an appropriate, competent, professional strategic planner from today's increasingly competitive market is a challenge. However, a systematic approach to this process can aid in the selection.

REQUEST FOR PROPOSAL

Initially, it is important to determine what is to be included in the strategic plan. If no strategic plan presently exists, the request for proposal (RFP) will need to incorporate many factors to produce a comprehensive response. If a strategic plan is in place, this process may simply require assistance with revisions or modifications to the current written plan. Providing the bidding firms with a copy of the existing plan will allow them to offer an "apples for apples" proposal. Addressing specific areas for assistance allows the board to judge which proposal would best fit the needs of the bank or thrift.

LIST OF BIDDERS

Clearly, deciding who should receive the requests for proposal is a painstaking step in the selection process. Before you reinvent the wheel, check with colleagues and competitors to discern who they believe are worthy planners. Take the time to examine advertisements in banking and thrift trade journals, national publications for banks and trade associations, as well as independent magazines and periodicals.

Be sure to talk to competitors in and outside your geographic area. Your goal is to send out at least five requests for proposals. To ensure competitive bidding, make each bidder aware that other firms are bidding also. State a deadline for submission so that bids are received within a given period. Outline the particulars to be included in the proposal—again, so that an "apples to apples" comparison can be made.

RECEIPT OF PROPOSALS

First, compare each of the proposals to determine the specifics of what is being offered, the time each firm plans to take to accomplish the project, and the cost of each proposal. Develop a matrix to compare each proposal point by point and cost by cost. When all proposals are received, do assign someone to contact references to determine how well past customers have been assisted in the strategic planning process.

INTERVIEWING THE PLANNERS

Once all the proposals are received, two or three will probably stand out. After references are checked, schedule interviews for these planners, unless their consulting work or reputation is known to the board. Interviews may be accomplished in person or by phone. However, remember that some of these planners will require reimbursement for their time or at least their expenses if they are asked to travel any significant distance for this interview with no assurance that they will be the successful bidder. Since the board will be seeking focused advice from these professionals, they may even request remuneration for the interview process. Remember, as strategic planners, giving advice is how they make a living. Free advice is often worth what you pay for it.

SELECTING A PLANNER AND SETTING DEADLINES

The next step is to formally engage the strategic planner. This should be achieved with a written contract agreed upon by the bank or thrift's legal counsel. Unless otherwise modified by mutual agreement of all parties, the strategic planning engagement should state contract deadlines to be met. If deadlines are not met, a penalty should be assessed to the strategic planner (e.g., 10 percent of the total engagement contract if 1 to 30 days late; 20 percent if 31 to 60 days late). Make sure the strategic planning firm understands that it works for your financial institution, not vice versa.

Unfortunately, strategic planning often has a tendency to halt the forward momentum of a financial institution. As the strategic planning process moves along, it is not unusual for relevant questions to be answered with "Let's wait until the strategic plan is complete." Unless the strategic plan is completed quickly, it is possible to lose 3 to 6 months of momentum. It is for that reason that a schedule and penalties for failing to meet deadlines should be a part of the up-front contract.

STRATEGIC PLANNING COSTS

Remember, you get what you pay for. If a maximum of $3,000 is budgeted, do not expect a valuable, workable strategic plan. Although it is possible to retain the services of a former bank president who markets his or her services as a strategic planner—beware! Strategic planning takes proficient expertise and should accomplish the unique objectives of the particular institution for which it is being developed. An experienced consulting firm cannot complete a competent strategic planning project for $5,000. This does not mean that the engagement should cost $50,000 (although for large multibillion dollar institutions it could); it simply means that professional fees will be based on what is to be accomplished.

Although some significant savings can be achieved by developing the strategic plan internally, there are some not so obvious costs. A vice president who spends all or half his or her time working on the strategic plan, for as long as 6 months, will continue to collect a salary plus fringe benefits—at considerable expense to the institution. In addition, the vice president's duties will suffer if she or he is trying to do both jobs. However, an outside strategic planning firm could be retained for much less and complete the project in half that time.

Another approach to costs is as a percentage of annualized net income. Strategic planning costs should not exceed 3 to 5 percent of net income in any one fiscal year. Implementation of the strategic plan should result in a return on that investment. If that return does not materialize, the board receives no benefit from the strategic planning analysis.

Consequently, typical costs for an initial strategic plan should be in the area of $7,500 and $15,000 plus expenses. However, the more you want, the more it will cost. Use the bidding process to qualify appropriate component costs for such planning. Stay alert when it comes to expenses, and perhaps include a "not to exceed" figure in the RFP. Unlimited or unspecified expenses could result in costs that exceed those of the actual plan.

There is one other alternative—albeit not a sensible alternative. If the strategic plan is developed internally, a strategic planner, accounting firm, or law firm could be hired to analyze the plan and assist as a sounding board. The initial cost is less, but ultimately the process will not be as effective. However, any strategic planning is better than none.

THE COST OF A STRATEGIC PLANNING RETREAT

A strategic planning retreat is usually a one-day to two-day event and should cost between $2,000 and $5,000. The aggregate amount will depend on how far the strategic planner travels and advance arrangements for the retreat (resulting in lower air fares, etc.). Assuming a cost of $5,000 for the services of the strategic plan facilitator is a practical "ball park" figure. If it is decided that the strategic planner will also write up the draft strategic plan after the retreat, that would be an additional $2,000 to $3,000, based upon what is requested. If a facilitator requests $10,000 to $20,000, competitive bidding for the retreat will keep expenses under control. A more detailed discussion of the strategic planning retreat and the role of the outside strategic planner will be discussed in Chapter 13.

EVALUATION OF THE STRATEGIC PLANNING PROCESS

One final step is important in the strategic planning process. If the services of a strategic planner will be used over the long run, the process and quality of strategic planning performed by the planner should be evaluated at the initial stages. Based on the planner's performance, or lack of performance, using another planner to vary the approach and results might be advisable. It is important to determine whether the financial institution received quality strategic planning services. If not, as the strategic planning process matures, the planner may need to be replaced. However, if results are favorable and the institution benefits, using the same planner can provide continuity, expertise, and greater knowledge to the strategic planning process. Thus, an objective and candid evaluation of the strategic planning process is important—not only after the initial engagement, but yearly as the plan is revised and modified.

SUMMARY

Strategic planning is essential to the survival of a community bank or thrift and it does not need to result in exorbitant costs.

Establish the needs of the financial institution, then, to lower the costs, competitively bid the strategic planning process.

A financial institution that pays too much for its strategic plan has failed to do the necessary homework. Establish a time schedule and make sure that the planner conforms to the schedule. Although the expertise of an experienced planner will help achieve the goals and objectives of the plan, successful strategic planning depends on how efficiently the engagement is handled by the financial institution (not the planner).

Remember, without a map, if you do not know where you are going, any road will do.

CHAPTER 8

The Role of the Board of Directors and Management in Strategic Planning

The board of directors is an elected group of individuals who are responsible to the shareholders. In the case of mutual savings and loan associations and mutual savings banks, the board of trustees has a fiduciary responsibility to the creditors and members of the association. From a practical perspective, these responsibilities in terms of strategic planning are not vastly different from banks. At the annual meeting of the shareholders, the shareholders elect the board of directors and, on occasion, even fire them. Regardless of the kind of organization, the board of directors is responsible to the shareholders for overall performance and safety and solvency. The board of directors delegates the day-to-day operations to the professional management. In many jurisdictions, and under most circumstances, management which is not performing satisfactorily may be fired with or without cause. In case of illegal and/or illicit activities, management may be suspended and/or fired immediately. In community banks or thrifts, the management and the board of directors may consist of the same individuals. In some cases, a board member(s) may also be the majority stockholder.

In the strategic planning process, the management performs the duties necessary to meet the objectives and goals of the board of directors. Generally, the board of directors will delegate to management the task of developing recommendations for general and specific strategic plans for approval by the board of directors. It cannot be overstated that the board of directors is not an everyday managerial unit of the community bank. The board of directors is a policymaking and decisionmaking body, and management is a performance-delegating body for the everyday operation of the bank. Strategic planning will fail without cooperation between management and the board of directors.

MANAGEMENT: RESPONSIBLE FOR STRATEGIC PLANNING MODIFICATION

More than any other individual or group, the management of a community bank or thrift is attuned to the effectiveness of strategic planning policies. It is, therefore, management's responsibility to suggest modifications, or outright elimination, of strategic planning policies. As management is accountable for the effectiveness of the implemented strategic plans, it also makes common sense for management to be responsible for modifications of any ineffective strategic policies.

PUTTING THE BOARD IN CHARGE

For purposes of this discussion, we will make an assumption that the board of directors is strong, and professional management is competent. In this scenario, the board of directors accepts its position in the planning process and serves as the overall policymaking constituency of the bank or thrift. The strategic planning process is initiated by the board of directors and delegated to management. The board of directors outlines as specifically as possible exactly what strategic planning tasks should be undertaken and the criteria for reports returned to the board. Management may accomplish the job internally or with the assistance of outside professional consultants. Although this preferred format is not common, a number of community bank and thrift boards are becoming more aware of their responsibilities and charging management with the preparation of strategic plans for approval by the board of directors.

RESPONSIBILITY TO THE BOARD

Whether the board or management has initiated the strategic planning process, it is management's responsibility to ensure that the job is done accurately. The job is to determine the future course of the institution and to cover all individual aspects sufficiently so the strategic plan has a probability of success within the constraints of the bank or thrift's ability to perform the strategic plan. Management should undertake a systematic analysis of the strategic planning process and develop a logical, rational plan that covers necessary areas.

INITIAL VERSUS ANNUAL STRATEGIC PLANNING

Almost exclusively, the initial strategic plan is accomplished by the board of directors and senior management. Junior management and staff are normally not informed of the goals and objectives of the institution and would be of little advantage in the development of the initial strategic plan. However, as the strategic plan matures, it is disseminated down through the ranks of the financial institution. As annual review and revisions are made, expanded information is offered from departments and functional divisions within the financial institution, thus allowing the strategic plan to become more valuable. Please note that as discussed in this book, strategic planning for a community banking organization defines a community bank as a financial institution of under $300 million in size. This often means that fewer than 100 people all total are employed, and many of them are line tellers and clerks who would not be involved in policy setting.

Once the board of directors has approved the annual strategic plan, management strategic planning, which includes the annual budget as well as departmental and divisional action plans for the next year, may take place. Functional strategic action plans for individual departments and divisions can be implemented in correlation with overall strategic planning. A board of directors will often request input from departments and divisions regarding their priorities. However, bottom-up strategic planning does not always result in achievement of focused goals and objectives. Thus, it is appropriate to plan downward from the financial institution's overall strategic plan to departmental and divisional actions plans within the institution to effectively and efficiently implement the overall plan.

ROLE OF DEPARTMENT HEADS AND STAFF

Participation by department heads and staff in the initial strategic plan is relatively limited. Department heads and staff often do not have an overall vision of the bank or bank holding company. They are very involved in operation functions, know their jobs intimately, and are well experienced in taking care of problems within their departments. However, this limited perspective restricts any significant assistance they might be able to offer in analysis and development of overall goals and objectives. However, the department managers become extremely helpful once the plan has been developed. Implementation of the strategic plan is typically accomplished at department levels.

As the strategic plan is reviewed, revised, and implemented year after year, the contribution by department heads becomes a more integral part of the planning process. As the planning process matures, involvement of department heads is based on their ability to determine how to meet the financial and nonfinancial goals and objectives through improved operations of their departments, innovations in product development and managerial expertise.

Realistically, complete bottom-to-top strategic planning in most community banks is not recommended owing to a lack of expertise of department heads and staff. Our recommendation is top-to-bottom strategic planning that is initially accomplished by the board of directors, senior management, and outside strategic planning consultants. Once the strategic plan has been outlined and defined, contributions toward the implementation may be encouraged by department heads and staff. If the level of experience or expertise of department heads is not sufficient, their assistance may actually hinder the overall attainment of goals and objectives.

As a case in point, one strategic planning engagement involved senior management of a $150 million community banking organization who authorized 14 department heads to develop goals and objectives for their departments. Senior management then attempted to consolidate the departmental strategic plans into an overall bank holding company strategic plan. Unfortunately, the results were disastrous. First, the 14 departmental plans included 14 different degrees of expertise. Some departmental plans were quite excellent and exquisite in detail and overall thought, while several other plans were less than 2 pages in length and exhibited a lack of administrative thoughtfulness or expertise. Second, each departmental strategic plan focused exclusively on that particular department and failed to interrelate with any other departments within the institution. Third, the accumulated information between departments had significant financial and nonfinancial gaps in both financial condition and expertise of personnel. The plans were mutually incompatible, and the goals and objectives of one department could only be achieved at significant disadvantage to other departments.

Fortunately, this story has a better than expected ending. A consulting firm assisted the bank holding company in developing goals and objectives and specific action plans to meet the goals and objectives—the general framework that the department managers had agreed upon. The strategic planning framework was then given to the department heads to establish departmental action plans to meet the bank financial and nonfinancial goals and objectives. Working together, each of the 14 departments knew exactly what must be done to meet its goals and objectives. The departments were able to agree upon the specific action plans necessary for implementation, transferring personnel, limiting duplicated operations and administration, developing new products and services, eliminating inefficiencies within and among departments, and attaining an overall team approach to meeting the goals and objectives. In this case, the bottom-to-top approach only did not work. However, once the overall framework was achieved, the expertise of the department heads was used to accomplish a top-to-bottom approach. It is imperative to know the organization well in order to determine which framework will work.

ONGOING STRATEGIC PLANNING DEVELOPMENT

Senior management should delegate the job of revising specific strategic plans to department managers as well as outside parties. The following steps should be taken by senior management to facilitate the orderly development and implementation of the strategic plan:

1. Senior management outlines specific bank goals and objectives to be accomplished. Department management must understand these goals.
2. Inform the management and staff of their duties and responsibilities to assist in the strategic planning process and its implementation.
3. Coordinate the efforts of department managers, staff, and senior officers in the development of department planning and reporting.
4. Within the constraints set by the board of directors, establish a timetable for submission of department plans and reports to the executive in charge of the planning process.
5. Senior management should receive proposed department plans 5 days prior to the final department plan deadline.
6. Changes in department plans should be made by appropriate senior management.
7. All final department plans must be submitted 3 to 5 days prior to the board of directors meeting for analysis.
8. All department plans should be acted on by the board or returned for additional information.

UTILIZING OUTSIDE CONSULTANTS

If the management of your financial institution is not planning oriented, does not have the experience, or does not have the time to work on planning, the use of outside strategic planning assistance is highly recommended. Outside expertise can be extremely valuable in developing initial strategic plans that will benefit your institution. Outside assistance can also help focus and make more efficient annual revisions to an existing strategic plan.

SUMMARY

Management has the responsibility for performing the strategic planning analysis or supervising its delegation to an outside planning group. Management is also responsible for the implementation of the strategic plan after it has been approved by the board of directors. Furthermore, as the strategic planning process matures, increased involvement of departmental and divisional management and staff becomes more significant to the sophistication and efficiency of the strategic plan. Finally, the time frame for strategic planning is relatively short. To minimize any interruption in forward momentum, strategic planning must become an efficient, short-term, annual process.

CHAPTER 9

Developing a Corporate Vision and Mission

In the first part of this book, we have discussed the impact of economic, regulatory, and financial conditions affecting community bank strategic plans. Through both an internal as well as an external analysis, we have identified strengths, weaknesses, opportunities, and threats. We have discussed the importance of a valuation for determining financial performance and its impact upon incentive compensation and evaluating the performance of senior management, and we have determined the role of the board of directors and the role of senior management in strategic planning. Finally, we have discussed how much it should cost to strategic plan and how to select a strategic planning planner to assist in the endeavor.

THE CORPORATE VISION

It is now time to actually begin to develop the strategic plan. We start with the development of a vision for the institution.

Remember that strategic planning encompasses a thought process that is futuristic and comprehensive. Developing a vision for the future of the financial institution is an essential step in the strategic planning process. The vision is a long-term projection of where you see the bank in the future. The written corporate vision is more than simply a mission or a short-term view of the future. The vision quantifies where an organization is going or the direction it should be headed in the 21st century. As such, strategic planning goals and objectives become a part of the corporate vision.

To develop this vision you must consider the following kinds of future issues that will face the financial institution:

1. How large will the institution become in 20 years?
2. How many offices will it operate?
3. What types of products and services will be provided?
4. What type of technology will be utilized to provide products and services?
5. Will this institution still exist or will it sell?
6. If the institution is a stock corporation, do the shareholders need to liquidate their stock (i.e., are they relatively old and need a more liquid investment). Can the stock be bought with resources from the bank or bank holding company or the thrift or thrift holding company?

These are merely a few of many questions that should be considered by directors and managers when determining the future course of a financial institution far into the future. Each will impact your institution, the industry, and the competition.

It is a safe bet that bankers like John B. McCoy (Banc One) or John Reed (Citicorp) have already developed their corporate vision and will be working toward that vision over the next 20 years. They have identified where they want to go and how to get there, based upon the current conditions faced by their organization. They hope to get there, knowing that they will need to modify their paths often over the next 20 years.

There is no reason that a smaller community bank or thrift cannot do the same thing. In fact, today's community bank may become a multistate, multibank organization within the next 20 years. Banc One was not always a $122.4 billion (assets) banking organization. In the mid 1970s it was an institution with less than $2.0 billion in assets. In 1970, First of America, headquartered in Kalamazoo, Michigan, was barely $300 million in size. However, by the end of 1996, assets were in excess of $25 billion. Twenty-five years from now, with a strong vision, a $100 million to $300 million community bank could be $25 billion in size. Your vision may only be to continue to provide quality financial services to the community. This corporate vision is just as relevant as attempting to become one of America's largest 200 financial institutions. What is important is that your corporate vision should be appropriate for your organization and your community.

Whether you are a commercial bank, thrift, or another depository or nondepository institutuon, you should have a corporate vision. Certainly, each institution's vision should be different. A vision should be appropriately specific for each individual financial institution. Your vision should not be a rehash of another institution's vision.

Also remember that the corporate vision should not be too specific. It should be a veil of illusion that encompasses desires and ambitions for 20 years into the future. Many factors will have an impact upon planned activities and therefore your vision should be redefined yearly. The corporate vision should be a written document. However, it is not suggested that the vision be disseminated to shareholders (if applicable), depositors and creditors, borrowers, or the community. The vision is for the board's use to direct where you plan to go, how you plan to get there, who you plan to out-compete, and who you plan to merge and acquire, and so on. The corporate vision must be set forth prior to the development of the corporate mission.

DIFFERENCES BETWEEN A VISION AND A MISSION

As mentioned earlier, the corporate vision is something to be kept inside the board room and in the minds of the directors and senior management. It should be placed on paper and revised annually just as the corporate mission should be.

In contrast, the mission is by its very nature more public relations–oriented. The mission could consist of simply a motto such as "Quality Service" or "First National—a Financial Leader." The mission could also be extensive enough to fill several pages. More commonly, it consists of one or two paragraphs outlining the philosophy and treatment of the community as an important player in the future of the financial institution. This mission is designed to be disseminated through financial statement stuffers, lobby counter cards, letterhead, annual reports, as well as newsletters to shareholders and customers of the financial institution. This document is also distributed to employees and becomes a part of their banking culture. Employees should be knowledgeable of the corporate mission and be able to explain it to customers, shareholders, and members of the community. In essence, a corporate mission is the public explanation and philosophy of a financial institution as it relates to the community, shareholders, customers, and staff.

THE CORPORATE MISSION

Every corporate mission should include at least six components:

1. *Discussion of financial performance objectives.* The corporate mission outlines the goals for financial performance and condition. Is the institution's aim to achieve a CAMELS 1 or MACRO 1 rating or is a rating of 2 satisfactory? If the institution is comfortable with a CAMELS or MACRO 2 rating or a Satisfactory rating for CRA and Consumer Compliance but wishes to maintain a 1.5 percent rate of return on assets and a 15 percent rate of return on equity—include those goals and objectives in the corporate mission.

2. *Emphasis on rates of return to shareholders (if applicable).* If the financial institution is a stock corporation, this component is a corollary of the first issue. In spite of what regulators believe, the ultimate owners of a financial institution are its shareholders, not the regulators, the community, or self-interest neighborhood groups. Thus, the corporate mission should indicate that the institution works for a fair return to its owners, which benefits the community.

3. *Competition within the marketplace.* Competition is another important part of the corporate mission statement. It should state the names and types of institutions who compete in your market and where the competition is located. For example, is the institution a full-service department store of financial services, or is it a boutique business and professional oriented commercial bank? Outline the specifics in the corporate mission so that customers are clear about what the financial institution is and is not.

4. *Communities to be served.* Outline areas to be served by the financial institution. This is important. As with the Community Reinvestment Act area, the financial institution is held responsible for competing within the area outlined. It is important to reach beyond the boundaries of the local community or even cross several state lines to show that the financial institution is a regional banking organization. The greater the distance from your hometown, the more expansive the philosophy and viewpoint can become. This could eliminate major problems of parochialism and mercantilism if the mission states that the financial institution is simply the "First National Bank of Plain City."

5. *Products and services offered.* The fifth element of the corporate mission is to discuss what products and services are to be offered. Products and services offered must be commensurate with the type of institution. If first mortgage, commercial, or consumer loans are not offered, say so in the corporate mission. Customers need to know whether they can utilize the services offered before they walk through the door or call on the phone.

6. *Remaining independent or positioning to sell.* Somewhere in the corporate mission (as well the corporate vision), the financial institution should state whether it plans to remain an independent community bank or thrift or if it plans to sell in the next 5 years. Selling out is not immoral and is one valid alternative available to shareholders and the board of directors. Thus, if it is determined that the financial institution would be better served by selling to achieve the best rate of return for shareholders, then the corporate mission should reflect that decision. Out of over 100 strategic plans, in only one instance has the corporate mission statement indicated that the bank for which we were consulting was attempting to package the bank for sale. Needless to say, it was not a long wait for interested bidders coming in the door. However, if the financial institution wishes to remain independent, even fiercely so, then the mission statement should say so, up front and confidently, and even repeatedly so that any conversion sharks or sale speculators will leave the institution alone. Acquirers are on the prowl for the weak, timid, and uncertain. If it is stated that plans are to remain autonomous and independent and that the financial institution does not wish to sell for the next 10 years, and your controlling shareholders do not want to sell, conversion sharks and sale speculators will go in search of a smaller and weaker target.

SAMPLE CORPORATE MISSION STATEMENTS

On the next three pages are actual (though sanitized) corporate mission statements. You will note that some corporate mission statements are relatively short. Succinct wording is the norm.

THE CORPORATE MISSION IS IMPORTANT—BUT IT IS NOT AN ENTIRE CAREER

For the last 30 years, working with community banks and thrifts to develop strategic plans has been a major part of our consulting business. In the last 5 years, one laughable consequence has occurred repeatedly—the corporate mission statement becomes the focal point of the strategic planning process. Arriving at the strategic planning retreat, I discover that for 2 days the board of directors and senior management have been debating over the wording of the corporate mission. A two-paragraph mission has consumed 10 to 12 hours of heated discussion. Do not misunderstand—it is important that the philosophy of the financial institution should be short, snappy, and memorable, but it need not be the Gettysburg Address.

Set aside a prescribed period of time to work on the corporate vision statement and the corporate mission statement, and do not exceed that time limit. The vision and mission can be word-smithed next year when the strategic plan is reviewed. In fact, by next year it is possible that the mission will need to be reconstructed simply because of

The mission of this bank is to provide its shareholders with a safe, profitable return on their investment, over the long term. Management will attempt to minimize risk to our shareholders by making prudent business decisions, will maintain adequate levels of capital and reserves, and will maintain effective communication with shareholders. It is our intention to promote the image of a locally owned, independent bank to the communities we serve, and to be a business that renders high-quality service to customers.

This bank was established to make a profit while serving the financial needs of our community, its businesses, and its citizens. We are in the financial services business, and no line of financial services is beyond our charter as long as it serves the needs of businesses and families in our community. We will aggressively analyze our financial market area on a continual basis and offer needed financial services to all business and social groups found in all income levels, without compromising standards of safety and soundness.

The bank is a responsible citizen and a business leader of the community. The bank takes its citizenship duties seriously and will not knowingly take actions that are adverse to the best interests of the community, its businesses, or its families.

The bank's most important asset is its customers. We will consider their needs first when we design our products, set our hours, and employ personnel. High-quality customer service is an important mission of this bank. How well we accomplish this mission will have a direct influence on our profitability.

Another important asset of our bank is the employees. Without dedicated and knowledgeable employees, it would be impossible for the bank to render high-quality customer service, and to be a contributing citizen to the community. The intent, therefore, is to be a responsible employer. All bank employees will be treated with dignity and respect. They will

Continued

be provided with the necessary training and education to perform their duties with confidence and professionalism. Management will take steps to encourage employees to become self-motivated in their work and to increase self-development. These qualities are recognized as being invaluable and contribute much to career advancement. All employees will be given equal opportunity and a fair wage without respect to race, color, sex, age, or physical handicap.

■ ■ ■

The bank, as the wholly owned subsidiary of the bank holding company has the corporate mission of maximizing shareholder value for its owners and acting as the financial leader for the communities it serves as a locally owned, independent community banking organization. Through the provision of high-quality, modern, progressive, and a complete line of products and services, the bank attempts to meet the financial needs of its customers. Provision of such services is grounded on the quality service provided by competent professional employees of the bank who are valued for their expertise, service, personality. These employees are provided by the bank with a high quality of living which prompts enthusiastic and motivational service to the community and customers they serve.

■ ■ ■

The bank is an independent, community bank dedicated to developing long-term customer relationships through high-quality, customer-valued products and services that will generate outstanding performance and profit.

■ ■ ■

Since the current wholly owned subsidiary affiliates of the holding company operate in such proximity to each other that the service areas are either adjacent to or are intermingled with each other, it was felt by the holding company

Continued

> participants that a single corporate mission for all the banks would suffice. Though operating independently and autonomously as much as possible, all affiliates are tied together integrally with each other as affiliates of the holding company and operate in such a fashion to meet the needs and conveniences of the public to be served without falling over each other and getting into each other's way. Thus, the corporate mission of the banks is by necessity the same so as to provide continuity and consistency among the banks and the people to be served.

changes in market conditions, new products and services offered, or even new federal and state legislation impacting upon the financial institution. The balance of the strategic planning process—such as establishment of financial and nonfinancial goals and objectives and implementation—are far more important than the vision and the mission.

SUMMARY

The corporate vision and mission statements of the strategic plan are indicative of the future planning and philosophy of the financial intermediary. The corporate vision statement is more ethereal, elusive, and subject to interpretation than the corporate mission, but it should be designed to assist the financial institution far beyond the time when the current board of directors is serving the institution.

In contrast, the corporate mission statement is a public relations document. The mission statement should be known by the staff as well as customers, shareholders, and the community. It is the official public expression of the financial institution's position. It should be modified on an annual basis, if necessary, and should be publicly discussed by the board, management, and through the annual meeting, etc., in order to clearly communicate your philosophical and operational direction to your constituencies.

CHAPTER 10

Establishing Goals and Objectives

The terminology *goals and objectives* is used interchangeably. They have no special meaning in this book other than to indicate future conditions and performance not yet achieved. Prior to establishing goals and objectives, it is important to understand that there are certain philosophical parameters that must be outlined. Goals and objectives must be:

- Achievable
- Realistic
- Pragmatic
- Based upon historical facts and current conditions, not impulses and whim
- In accordance with the basic business philosophy of the community bank
- Evaluated, reappraised, and reapproved every year

It is unreasonable to develop goals and objectives that cannot be achieved through competent performance by the community bank. Do not expect unattainable goals and objectives to be reached in the immediate future. For example, if the bank is earning 0.6 percent rate of return on average assets (ROAA), an objective of 1.75 percent established for next year is probably not realistic, pragmatic, or achievable. However, if a 0.7 percent ROAA is a goal for next year, that is a realistic and achievable objective. Unattainable goals and objectives position management for failure year after year. Small annual steps to achieve desired long-term goals and objectives are much more realistic.

Boards also face the challenge of a cultural philosophy to regularly increase goals and objectives. By way of illustration, if the institution is earning 1.6 percent rate of return on average assets, and peer groups are earning 1.2 percent, then it may be inappropriate to establish a goal and objective of 1.7 to 1.8 percent ROAA. A wiser approach is a goal of maintaining a 1.6 percent rate of return, or, alternatively phrased, establishing an ROAA goal in excess of 1.6 percent annually. The same would be true of capital adequacy. If the institution maintains a 12 percent capital ratio and peer groups have achieved an 8.5 percent capital ratio, it is best to establish the goal of a capital ratio in excess of 10 percent. Do not feel compelled to improve every year, especially if performance is already significantly above average. It is essential that goals and objectives be based upon past performance and the financial condition of the community bank. Performance improvements can be made, or the same level of performance can be maintained. Goals and objectives must have a correlation to what has been done in the past.

At the same time, goals and objectives must be in line with the financial institution's business philosophy. An abrupt focus on commercial lending as a goal in an institution with a small commercial loan pool and limited commercial lending experience or expertise would be a major mistake. Remain true to the financial institution's culture, and make sure that goals and objectives are in line.

It is important to understand that goals and objectives will change over time. As the industry changes, goals and objectives will change. As the competition changes within the market, goals and objectives will change. As financial performance improves, goals and objectives will be better focused and become more valuable. Accordingly, it is necessary to analyze established goals and objectives, confirm their appropriateness, or modify them. If this is done on an annual basis, goals and objectives will remain current and relevant to the future performance of the institution.

Goals and objectives also should be broken out into financial goals and objectives and nonfinancial goals and objectives. Financial goals and objectives indicate specific growth rates, performance levels, and financial ratios to be achieved. Nonfinancial goals and objectives generally refer to all other goals and objectives regarding competitive, managerial, industry, and other issues facing the institution. This is not to say that nonfinancial goals and objectives have no financial impact. In fact, achievement of nonfinancial goals and objectives will result in direct and indirect financial costs (and hopefully income enhancement) both as they are implemented and into the future (for example, the introduction of a new product or service). The development and roll-out of the product or service would initially entail increased expense. However, the goal of this new product would be to increase income over time. The financial impacts of nonfinancial goals and objectives, therefore, should be factored into financial goals and objectives when established.

FINANCIAL GOALS AND OBJECTIVES

Establishing financial goals and objectives should be based primarily on past financial performance and current financial condition. Financial goals and objectives are based also upon the desires of the board of directors and senior management. Table 10-1 outlines a format for establishing financial goals and objectives. Please note that financial goals and objectives are determined for each year in the planning horizon. Each year, as the strategic plan is revised, the past year is replaced by one year into the future. Not all the listed financial goals and objectives will be relevant for every community bank or thrift. For example, the dividend payout ratio is not applicable to a mutual savings and loan or mutual savings bank. However, these financial goals and objectives are indicative and illustrative of what should be reviewed and set as a standard for the years to come. If certain financial issues are not addressed on this list, simply create a specific list for your financial institution to analyze and set goals and objectives.

NONFINANCIAL GOALS AND OBJECTIVES

It is impossible to categorize all the different nonfinancial goals and objectives that a financial institution may need to explore. Each community bank or thrift has different needs and requirements and faces different competitive factors. The strengths and weaknesses of each organization may be entirely different. As Table 10-2 shows, there are certain basic nonfinancial objectives that an institution may wish to examine to determine if this is a priority at their institution. The nonfinancial goals and objectives outlined in Table 10-2 may not be appropriate for every community bank or thrift. Further, there may be some nonfinancial aspects of your operations that are not included on this list. In all cases, nonfinancial goals and objectives should be established for each year in the planning horizon similar to financial goals and objectives.

TABLE 10-1

Situation Analysis

Financial Goals and Objectives	1998	1999	2000
Rate of return on average assets	______	______	______
Rate of return on average equity	______	______	______
Earnings per share*	______	______	______
Dividend payment ratio*	______	______	______
Net interest margin	______	______	______
Net interest income as a percent of total assets	______	______	______
Risk based capital to assets ratio	______	______	______
Regulatory capital to assets	______	______	______
Tier 1/tier 2 capital	______	______	______
Allowance for loan and lease losses	______	______	______
Provision for loans and lease losses	______	______	______
Past due loans—30–90 days	______	______	______
Past due loans—90+ days	______	______	______
Nonaccrual loans	______	______	______
Fee structured and renegotiated loans	______	______	______
Charge-off loans	______	______	______
OREO (ORE)	______	______	______
Loans to total assets	______	______	______
Loans to total deposits	______	______	______
Liquidity ratio	______	______	______
Overhead ratio	______	______	______
Efficiency ratio	______	______	______
CAMELS (MACRO) rating	______	______	______
CRA rating	______	______	______
Consumer compliance rating	______	______	______

* Not applicable for mutual associations

TABLE 10-2

Situation Analysis

Nonfinancial Goals and Objectives	1998	1999	2000
Organizational structure (organization chart)	______	______	______
Management succession	______	______	______
Management replacement	______	______	______
Management retructuring	______	______	______
New senior management needed	______	______	______
Director succession	______	______	______
Director replacement (resignation and removal)	______	______	______
New director recruitment	______	______	______
Management education	______	______	______
Staff education and training	______	______	______
Director education	______	______	______
Internal growth through deposit rates	______	______	______
External growth through purchase of branches	______	______	______
External growth through sale of branches	______	______	______
External growth through mergers and acquisitions	______	______	______
External growth through purchase of or commencement of operations of nonbanking subsidiaries	______	______	______
Sale of mutual funds, annuities, and other nonbanking products such as insurance, real estate brokerage	______	______	______
Development of new products and services—mutual funds; annuities; insurance (all types); brokerage (all types); real estate; investment advice; equipment leasing	______	______	______

Continued

TABLE 10-2

Continued

Nonfinancial Goals and Objectives	1998	1999	2000
Technology			
Internal versus outsourced computerization	______	______	______
LANS and WANS informal systems	______	______	______
Networking of all internal computers	______	______	______
EFTs	______	______	______
POS	______	______	______
Home banking—telephone/computer	______	______	______
Imaging technology	______	______	______
Loan operations computerized loan applications and documentation	______	______	______
ATMs	______	______	______
Updated policies and procedures manuals (required by regulators)	______	______	______
Days and hours of service			
Main lobby	______	______	______
Branch lobby	______	______	______
Drive-through	______	______	______

SUMMARY

Without a doubt, the most important part of strategic planning will be outlining the specific financial and nonfinancial goals and objectives. This chapter assists in determining the types of financial and nonfinancial goals and objectives for forecasting with recommendations that they be achievable, realistic, and pragmatic. Each community bank and thrift is different. What is important for one institution may not be important for another. Thus, flexibility is a major requirement for development of strategic planning goals and objectives. As will be discussed in the next chapter, achieving established goals and objectives will depend upon the implementation of those goals and objectives.

CHAPTER 11

Implementing Goals and Objectives through Strategic Action Plans

The development of either financial or nonfinancial goals and objectives is immaterial unless they are implemented through specific action plans. Strategic action plans are proposed by management and approved by the directors of the financial institution. Implementation of action plans is the next to last step in strategic planning.

Implementing goals and objectives is critical to the overall strategic planning process. The purpose of formalizing strategic action plans is to achieve the goals and objectives. Action plans should be specific, detailed, and assigned to an individual or group who will be held accountable for implementation by the board of directors. A strategic plan can easily fail after defining the goals and objectives if action plan implementation and accountability of management and/or board members are not achieved and established.

THE THREE PILLARS OF IMPLEMENTATION

The first pillar of implementation for strategic action plans is *prioritization.* The financial and nonfinancial goals and objectives discussed in Chapter 10 have not been given any prioritization. It is the responsibility of the board of directors and senior management to establish such priorities. Limited resources prohibit all action plans from being achieved in a given year. Consequently, the action plans must be reprioritized each year. When strategic planning is addressed next year, goals and objectives are again subject to reprioritization. A goal that had a priority of fifth last year may be moved up to first priority or down to a priority of eighth next year, depending on changing circumstances. The process is not as simple as checking down the list until all of last year's priorities have been achieved. When next year's strategic planning review takes place, all goals and objectives are open again to reprioritization.

The second pillar is *realism.* Establish only the number of action plans that can realistically be accomplished in each year. In our experience, the more action plans scheduled for implementation by management and staff in each year, the fewer action plans will actually be accomplished. Thus, the strategic plan will be less efficient. If 3 or 4 priorities are specified, chances are they can be achieved. If 20 priorities are identified, many of them will not be accomplished. Too many priorities impact upon the ability of management and staff to carry on current duties. For example, a strategic action plan we reviewed several years ago indicated that 14 task forces were to be set up after the strategic plan was developed. A banker friend of mine was chair of 7 of those task forces and a member of 12 of the 14. When asked how things were going, he said that for the last 6 weeks, he had not been near his desk to perform his regular duties. While he was involved in all the task forces, the current business of the bank was not being accomplished! Needless to say, there were too many action plans to be implemented at one time.

The third pillar of implementation is *accountability.* Management team members should be assigned responsibility for implementation of specific action plans. If the assigned goals and objectives do not get implemented, those individuals should be held accountable. The most effective way to hold management accountable is to establish a review process ex poste to ensure that the individuals and/or their teams have implemented the action plans as established. Obviously, this may need to be modified over time, and there may be good business reasons for action plans not being fully implemented. For instance, certain action plans may have to be revised to meet new circumstances. However, if management members are not held accountable for action plans ascertained by the board of directors in the strategic planning analysis, management members will not implement the action plans, and the strategic planning process will fail.

Table 11-1 is an example of a strategic action plan prioritization schedule. Please note that priorities for each of the next 3 years are listed on the left as well as the date of implementation and the individual responsible for such implementation.

SUMMARY

Implementation of financial and nonfinancial goals and objectives which arise from strategic planning can be accomplished only through a prioritization of realistic strategic action plans for which management will be held accountable. Implementation must be on an annual basis and be within the boundaries of staff members to realistically carry out. Strategic action plans must be prioritized in order to maximize opportunities to achieve the goals and objectives of the institution. Each year, during the strategic planning process or at the strategic planning retreat, the action plans must be reprioritized to ascertain whether last year's lower ranked prioritizations are still appropriate or must be changed.

TABLE 11-1

Strategic Action Plans—1998, 1999, 2000 for First National Bank

	Priorities Year One	Strategic Action Plan	Final Date of Implementation	Individual Responsible
1				
2				
3				
4				
5				
	Priorities Year Two	**Strategic Action Plan**	**Final Date of Implementation**	**Individual Responsible**
1				
2				
3				
4				
5				
	Priorities Year Three	**Strategic Action Plan**	**Final Date of Implementation**	**Individual Responsible**
1				
2				
3				
4				
5				

CHAPTER 12

Now That You Have a Strategic Plan, What Do You Do with It?

A written strategic plan is essential for today's financial institution. Interstate community bank regulators now insist on a written strategic plan, and members of the board of directors and senior management must utilize a strategic plan in order to know the future direction of their financial institution.

The industry has evolved. Initially, a community bank or thrift was encouraged to write a strategic plan. That suggestion has developed into a more significant issue of what should be done with the written strategic plan. About 10 years ago during a board of directors seminar in Ames, Iowa, only 3 of the 90 banks represented actually had written strategic plans. In contrast, a more recent presentation revealed that almost 85 percent of those in attendance had written strategic plans. However, when the bankers were asked what they had done with their strategic plans, a majority of responses were that once it was completed, the plan was shelved. Such a response from management is comparable to having no plan at all.

A strategic plan should not be drafted, approved, and then neglected. A strategic plan is a road map to the future survival of the financial institution. Taken literally, the road to survival is like a highway—constantly under construction. There are always repairs to be made, expansions for future routes, and unused avenues that are closed down.

A fundamental mistake of strategic planning is for the board and senior management to determine that because the plan was designed for 3 years, it does not need to be reviewed until the 3-year period expires. A 3-year period is much too long a time between revisions because of yearly changes in the banking industry. Priorities established in 1997 may not be relevant in 1998. Opportunities to act earlier or delay action due to changes in the industry or local conditions are common. Each written strategic plan must be flexible and amenable to change.

As we have discussed, we recommend a rolling 3-year planning horizon. For example, the 1998 planning session should include the years 1999, 2000, and 2001. At the end of 1999, the planning session would cover 2000, 2001, and 2002. On a rolling basis, drop the current year from the plan and add 1 year into the future. This should ensure that strategic planning is addressed every year—not just every 3 years.

THE YEARLY REVIEW

At least annually, the strategic plan should be analyzed and reviewed. A few financial institutions actually examine their strategic plan quarterly, but at most community banks and thrifts this would normally be unnecessary.

Hold nothing back during the annual review of the strategic plan. The plan has value only if there is total honesty and candid discussion of accomplishments, failures, and what is necessary for future survival. If current activities are whitewashed or simply rationalized, the strategic plan will have little value. It must be used as a tool from which to learn from past mistakes. Furthermore, the "big-picture" perspective must be taken into consideration, since the strategic plan encompasses not only current activity but also what should be done within the financial industry in order to survive. Ongoing comprehensive strategic planning indicates to the regulators that a financial institution is making an effort to do its best.

Annual review of the strategic plan also allows a way by which the board can evaluate senior management's performance. As part of the written plan, certain goals were established for the year. Some of these goals may have been assigned to senior managers. Accomplishing goals should be rewarded. If the annual review reveals that these goals have not been achieved by senior management, it should be determined why senior management has not accomplished them. Senior management should be held accountable and this performance or lack of performance in accomplishing goals should be reflected in senior management's evaluation. If senior management is allowed to slide, or the plan is not reviewed and analyzed in a timely manner, the goals will not be accomplished, and, ultimately, the responsibility comes back to the board.

PRIORITIZE AGAIN

When the strategic plan was initially developed, priorities for certain strategic action plans were identified for specific time frames. Enter the annual strategic planning process with the understanding that everything is open for discussion, debate, and change. This makes it possible to reprioritize strategic action plans for the upcoming year. For example, let's say an institution is located on the state border. In previous years, there has been no opportunity to branch across state lines. Along comes interstate branching reform. If it is now possible to cross state lines, deciding where to branch could change significantly. Because of the opportunity to make new choices, branching opportunities should be realigned to include out-of-state locations. To blindly follow previously determined branching priorities would be an imprudent business decision.

REVISING GOALS AND OBJECTIVES

It is necessary to remind the reader that the purpose of annual review of the strategic plan is to determine whether revision of the financial and nonfinancial goals and objectives previously set forth is necessary. If the review does not indicate that financial and nonfinancial goals and objectives need to be revised, then do not change them. On the other hand, be flexible enough to understand that some financial as well as the nonfinancial goals and objectives and their priorities will change owing to conditions within the financial institution as well as within the market.

IMPLEMENTING THE REVISED GOALS AND OBJECTIVES

Do not forget to implement new strategic action plans when revising financial goals and objectives. The former strategic action plans must be prioritized and possibly even eliminated. A new year brings new strategic action plans and new priorities. Furthermore, new priorities and new implementations bring new responsibilities to officers.

CRA ISSUES

The board of directors and senior management may or may not agree with the Community Reinvestment Act. In recent years, a growing number of financial institutions have set aside lending dollars for "risky" customers who would not be considered creditworthy under normal credit standards. These financial institutions have made it known that they will take certain risks (within a dollar range) that may never come back in the form of repayment of principal and interest. They put their community in the forefront of helping to develop neighborhoods and businesses and to assist individuals in obtaining needed credit.

Some profits may be sacrificed. However, when the compliance examiners arrive, the financial institution will be better served if CRA and fair credit guidelines are addressed proactively in the strategic plan. Utilize the strategic plan to assist in achieving CRA and compliance guidelines. Including CRA and fair credit in the annual strategic plan will show state and federal banking regulators that the financial institution considers equal opportunity lending a basic responsibility.

EVALUATING MANAGEMENT

One of the toughest jobs undertaken by directors is how to evaluate management competency and performance. Even state and federal banking regulatory agencies essentially utilize management as a qualitative rather than a quantitative factor. If a bank has a CAMELS rating of 3, it is possible that management may be the determining factor. It is not often that management is given a CAMELS rating of 1 with an overall CAMELS 3 rating for the bank. Furthermore, it is unlikely an institution would receive a CAMELS 1 rating with a CAMELS 3 in management. Bank directors must be able to judge management skills and performance, and an annual review of the strategic plan becomes an excellent source for that regular evaluation.

The written strategic plan is a road map for management and staff. At the end of the year, it allows the board to judge how well management has performed. There are established financial and nonfinancial goals. Specific objectives for management to accomplish are highlighted. Specific managers are linked with appropriate plans and will provide the information to evaluate how well they have done.

There may be legitimate reasons that certain plans are not accomplished. There will be instances where management exceeded expectations. Do not accept deviations from the written strategic plan without substantial scrutiny of management. The better the performance, the more competent the manager. A manager who does not meet the assigned objectives perhaps should not be given any additional managerial responsibilities. Such a manager may even need to be replaced with a more competent manager.

REMEMBER THE LONG TERM

Much too often, strategic planning done year after year, often becomes a business plan for only the next year. The board of directors and senior management must remember the long term. During one strategic planning retreat, a 50-page strategic plan was distributed by management to the board of directors. After reviewing the plan, comments were encouraged. At which point the number-one question was, "Where are the second and third years of the plan?"

The plan was essentially a 1-year business plan. Senior managers spent so much time making sure that the current year was addressed that they had truncated the long-term into 1 year. The world does seem to move more quickly today, and long-term may be next Tuesday. However, remember that the strategic plan should focus on where the financial institution will be 3 years from now.

SUMMARY

If done properly, strategic planning is never complete. To survive, a financial institution must constantly review what has already been accomplished and analyze what must be attained over the next several years. Strategic planning is the responsibility of the board of directors and senior management. Without a written strategic plan that is realistic and vibrant and that meets the needs of the community, your bank or thrift will not survive.

Now that you have a written strategic plan, what do you do with it? The answer is simple: Spend more time reviewing and revising the plan than was spent getting it started. Next year's written strategic plan will be better than the first year. The following year, the plan will be even better, more sophisticated, more detailed, and more relevant to accomplishments.

Strategic planning never stops. If there is a written strategic plan sitting on the shelf gathering dust, it is time to either update it and use it or sell out.

CHAPTER 13

The Strategic Planning Retreat

The strategic planning retreat held outside the bank or thrift is by far the most important annual planning session in which the board of directors is involved. It is not advisable to attempt strategic planning at regular monthly board meetings or at committee meetings. First, such meetings do not permit adequate time for in-depth strategic planning. Second, the atmosphere is not suitable for candid, honest, full discussions. Third, priority items that must be handled on a monthly basis limit any effective strategic planning discussion at a regular board meeting. Thus, the strategic planning retreat or meeting must be one of the major scheduled meetings of the year. It should be held strictly for the purpose of strategic planning with no other agenda. It should be scheduled at a time that all board members and appropriate management members can be in attendance. The strategic planning session must be a paramount priority. It is an important part of the year used to evaluate past and current events and to project controlling factors for sound operations and future strategic action plans.

LOCATION

An off bank premises location is recommended. If the strategic planning session is scheduled during business hours or if held on premises, there is no way for senior management as well as some directors to avoid interruptions. In 150-plus strategic planning retreats as facilitation leaders, the most ineffective have always been held in the financial institution during business hours and too close to phones and staff.

However, if the session is scheduled for a Saturday or Sunday (when the bank or thrift is closed), it is possible to work within familiar territory. Nevertheless, conversation flows much more freely and the atmosphere is more open if strategic planning is approached from a neutral location such as a local hotel or big-city major hotel complex or resort. A major advantage of an informal but structured planning session is the increase in camaraderie between directors and senior officers. Strategic planning retreats can be fun, and fun recreations should be scheduled such as golf, fishing, shopping, entertainment, and dining as detailed later in this chapter.

WHO SHOULD ATTEND

A strategic planning retreat should be attended by the appropriate people. How's that for a cop-out! Realistically, there have been some planning sessions which were attended by only the board of directors. At the other end of the spectrum, some community banks like to include all the directors plus every management member who carries the title "officer." The most efficient retreats are those where the board of directors meet with appropriate senior officers (those who might be called "Regulation O" officers or the policy officers). Over time, decisions can be made as to who should attend, but if there are no current policy officer roles within the institution, efforts should be made to arrange policy officer positions within a short time frame. In addition to the facilitator, other resources—such as legal counsel or the corporation's CPA—could be included to assist in the educational aspects of the retreat.

The objective is for candid, full disclosure and discussion of current significant topics as well as addressing important questions and issues into the future. Some of the discussions will not be pleasant—retirement of the president or even removal of a senior lending officer. Accordingly, planning retreats or sessions need not include extraneous personnel who do not have a full comprehension of all the issues. In addition, junior officers will often choose not to speak up in the presence of directors—and it is a fact that directors have a tendency not to talk in front of junior officers. In situations where the president of the bank or thrift insists that the planning session include everyone but the janitor, a 3- to 4-hour segment at the end of the program can be provided with discussions limited to only the board of directors on sensitive issues.

ATTENDANCE OF SPOUSES

If the board decides that this is appropriate, of course spouses should be invited to the retreat. There are boards who will argue that this is not the best way to spend the shareholders' money. To avoid any burden on the shareholders, a simple solution is for individual directors to personally pay the costs for his or her spouse. Having a spouse join the director or management member at the planning retreat, especially if it is held in a mid-city hotel or resort, makes the session a more pleasant experience and a perfect opportunity to be a part of the activities. Directors are more relaxed and, after working diligently on strategic planning, they can spend time with their spouses and new friends enjoying social amenities. The outcome can be better networking among directors and management that results in improved performance in years to come.

THE STRUCTURE OF THE RETREAT

The structure of a planning retreat or session can be comfortably flexible. The structure of the retreat should grow and change over time until it functions best for the institution. For educational purposes, there are a variety of commonly used structures for strategic planning retreats:

- One-day strategic planning retreat—often scheduled for 8:00 a.m. to 6:00 p.m.
- Night before and the morning of the following day planning retreat
- Two evenings in a row—perhaps 5:00 p.m. to 9:00 p.m.
- Two consecutive weekends—maybe Saturday mornings from 8:00 a.m. to noon
- Three half-day sessions—Friday, Saturday, Sunday at a resort with strategic planning in the morning, golf or other recreation in the afternoon

Each of these structures is workable, but why not make it fun as well as work? The board of directors does not often get together socially and probably seldom gets together with management. It is important for the board to know the management, especially as the retirement of current senior management nears. It will become necessary to promote leadership—either from inside the institution or from outside sources. Allowing the board to get to know junior and secondary senior management members will facilitate identification of suitable members on the staff who can get the job done in the next generation.

ILLUSTRATIVE AGENDA

Table 13-1 is an illustrative agenda for a strategic planning retreat. The agenda should be modified for particular circumstances. The agenda contemplates a full-day program with social time and dinner after the program.

The first educational session of the program is a review of what is going on in the economy and especially the banking industry and how that impacts upon your community bank or thrift. Utilizing an outside facilitator is especially beneficial for this overview. The second session is a review of the financial condition, performance trends of the bank or thrift, and comparing performance with peer group performance. This discussion should be candid and often is best handled by an objective outsider with no personal or emotional affiliation to the institution.

The next phase of the strategic planning session is to go through a complete situation analysis which indicates current strengths, weaknesses, opportunities, and threats to the institution. This session also includes a discussion of significant issues or hot topics. These issues are derived from a review of questionnaires sent to individual directors and senior management as well as information gleaned from the financial and nonfinancial information reviewed by the facilitator prior to the meeting. At this point, it should be noted that this facilitator requests 3 to 5 years of financial information, previous strategic plans, budgets, uniform bank performance reports, and often the aggregate examination results which enables the facilitator to become familiar with the current condition and past performance of the financial institution. From this information, any hidden agendas and any other significant issues not disclosed can be unearthed for discussion by the board of directors and management. The situation analysis is more easily accomplished if there is a written strategic plan to review and revise.

TABLE 13-1

Strategic Planning Retreat Agenda Suggestions

7:30–8:00	Continental breakfast
8:00–8:15	Introduction of facilitator [*Opening comments concerning facilitation retreat program and schedule.*]
8:15–9:00	Current aspects of community banking in your state and elsewhere [*This discussion will assist directors in focusing on the big picture of community banking and its impact on your bank and other banks throughout the United States. Discussion will include mergers/acquisitions, failures, fair credit, Community Reinvestment Act, investments under FASB 115, etc.*]
9:00–9:10	Break
9:10–10:00	Review of your bank's current position [*Open-ended discussion concerning current financial and nonfinancial aspects, noting current competitive posture of your bank vis-à-vis other banks in the market.*]
10:00–11:00	Current S-W-O-T [*This time will be set aside for reaffirming strengths, weaknesses, opportunities, and threats. You have done this in the past, and it has value, so it will be done again. Each year, the bank's SWOT changes, and this will bring us up to date and help us determine whether the bank 's strengths have improved, whether weaknesses have changed, etc.*]
11:00–11:15	Break
11:15–12:00	Vision and mission [*In 19XX, a corporate mission was developed for your bank. This session will discuss the vision for the bank over the next decade and whether the corporate mission is still viable.*]
12:00–1:00	Lunch [*This can be either participants only or include spouses—whatever you decide.*]
1:00–2:00	Financial and nonfinancial goals and objectives—1999–2001 [*Particular and specific financial and nonfinancial goals and objectives will be outlined for the board of directors and senior management—see sample format enclosed for your review. These are the types of goals and objectives to be discussed.*]
2:00–2:10	Break
2:10–3:30	Development of strategic plans for implementation of financial goals and objectives [*How do we get to goals and objectives specifically? How do we get there on time, and who is responsible for getting us there? This is the most important aspect of the strategic plan for 1999–2001.*]

Continued

TABLE 13-1

Continued

3:30–4:30	Overflow items [*If all agenda items are not covered, use this time to finish. This time could also be utilized for general questions and answers on topics not (necessarily) involving the strategic plan.*]

Once the situation analysis is complete, a review of the vision and corporate mission should be completed to identify any areas of change. The board of directors and senior management should then begin to establish financial and nonfinancial goals and objectives for the next 3 years. Finally, the strategic action plans are developed identifying responsible parties for implementation of financial and nonfinancial goals and objectives. This course of action provides a road map for the financial institution for the next 3 years with specific goals and objectives, individuals responsible for implementation, as well as a time frame for implementation.

PROCEDURAL ASPECTS

Some of the following procedural aspects of the strategic planning retreat may be of assistance:

1. Tape-record the strategic planning session in case anyone cannot attend the retreat. Some banks and thrifts will not hold a retreat unless every invited director or officer is in attendance. However, there are times when the tapes allow the retreat to be brought to the director or officer.

2. Recording the retreat will also assist senior management in remembering clearly what actually was decided. The tapes can also be utilized to assist in development of a written draft of the strategic plan.

3. Determine beforehand who will be responsible for drafting or revising the strategic plan: an outside party (such as the facilitator) or a management member.

4. Utilize outside professional assistance to provide educational sessions throughout the strategic planning retreat. These paid presentations assist the institution. By participating in the planning session, the consultants become more knowledgeable about the institution and the directors become more aware of the role these outsiders play.

5. During the planning session, make sure there is adequate time for conversations among the directors and management to discuss problems, suggestions, theories, principles, and ideas without impinging upon time deadlines.

6. Sometime during the strategic planning retreat, outside directors should meet without inside management. Inside management and the president or CEO should recognize this practice as a routine that will be done by directors as a matter of ordinary business.

7. Physical facilities for the retreat should have appropriate audio and visual equipment, flip charts, meeting rooms, and so on to make the retreat pleasant. As with any project, the better the tools, the more effective the results.

8. The facility should also have an excellent catering staff that provides above-average meals. Directors should be treated as royalty. Since they make many important decisions for the institution, keep them happy.

AFTER THE RETREAT

One of America's great philosophers, Yogi Berra, was reported to have said, "It's not over until it's over." When visualizing the strategic planning process, keep in mind that it is not over when it is over. It is not over until the revised, written strategic plan is in the hands of the board of directors, until it has been reviewed by them, and until the plan is approved for implementation for the next annual planning cycle. Only then is the strategic planning retreat and the annual strategic planning function over. Actually there is one remaining item to attend to—the strategic plan should be reviewed during the year if changes occur in the institution, the market, or the economy that was totally unanticipated by the board. The strategic planning document must be flexible enough to adapt to these changes.

SUMMARY

The annual planning retreat is one of the most important meetings the board of directors and senior management will attend each year. Consider the retreat an opportunity to refocus the future direction of the bank or thrift and an occasion for fellowship with other directors and management to create a better team that works together more effectively. The strategic planning retreat is the one opportunity annually to consider the big picture and to ask and answer significant questions facing the financial institution. It is the best time to think comprehensively and to project the future of your financial institution in a more efficient and productive manner. The strategic planning retreat is utilized for planning, not putting out fires, reacting to regulatory scrutiny, thwarting unsolicited takeovers, or overreacting to shareholders.

CHAPTER 14

Shareholders

Managers and directors of community banks and thrifts are often overwhelmed with problems of lenders' liability, disgruntled customers, and regulatory concerns. As a result, managers and directors may overlook shareholders, their most important constituency.

A key component of every strategic plan is to improve shareholder relations and communications so that shareholders will want to remain loyal to survival efforts of the financial institution. Survival does not depend on whether regulators, depositors, borrowers, or neighborhood associations believe that efforts are for their benefit. The potential to survive as a viable, profitable, and solvent institution depends upon satisfying the wishes and demands of shareholders.

This chapter offers a number of ways to improve shareholder relations and communications. These techniques differ significantly between "public" depository financial institutions and those institutions that are relatively "private" in nature. The methods in this chapter are confined to discussions of the community banking depository institutions, where Securities and Exchange Commission (SEC) rules and regulations do not apply, and where public scrutiny and banking analysts are not present to any significant degree. This limitation, however, does not diminish the significance of the topic since a majority, over 8,363 of the 9,451, of the community banks in this country have less than $300 million in assets.

Please note that this chapter does not address mutual thrifts. However, some of these tricks of the trade can be applied to mutual thrift members. Mutuals do not have shareholders demanding increased dividends or a higher stock price. When reading this chapter, assume that discussions apply no differently to thrift associations than a stock organization, without profitability and capital gain motives. Even without stock, most of these suggestions will improve member relationships and lead to a better relationship with customers.

SHAREHOLDER RELATIONS AND COMMUNICATIONS

Every banking institution should have a basic shareholder relations and communications program. The purpose of this program, first and foremost, is dissemination of financial information and the overall performance of the banking institution with management's discussion of same.

The second function of shareholder relations and communications is the sharing of information to and coordination with the media (including print, radio and television), so that information is fully disclosed and accurately portrayed.

The third function is to develop stronger shareholder relations and communications programs that favorably influence the media and shareholders. At the same time, this influence will carry over to the public so that financial and nonfinancial controversies and threats are viewed as opportunities for future success.

The fourth function is keyed to the development of strong shareholders meetings. A strong shareholders' meeting provides the banking organization with the best opportunity to portray itself as an excellent financial institution.

Finally, good shareholder relations and communications means being able to effectively handle adverse news such as operating losses, loan losses, embezzlements, frauds, or other problems. These situations should be handled in such a fashion that problems are fully disclosed and accurately portrayed to the public and yet explosive conditions within the marketplace are defused. Shareholder relations and communications functions cannot and should not portray the conditions as favorable, but as politicians would say, a solid shareholder relations and communications function can develop the appropriate "spin" control to minimize the negative impact of these conditions.

FIFTEEN KEYS TO SUCCESS

Key 1: Goals and Objectives for Shareholder Relations and Communications

Treat shareholder relations and communications like the favored stepchild in the management and direction of the banking organization. Plan carefully so that shareholder relations and communications will fit into the overall delivery of information on a regular basis. The board of directors should devise and implement appropriate goals and objectives for this area. Evaluate the strengths and weaknesses on a regular basis and make modifications to the plan. Remember, shareholders are your most important constituency.

Key 2: Shareholder Loyalty

Community banking organizations need the loyalty of their shareholders. In many community institutions, shareholders *are* loyal. Why else would shareholders retain their stock when the return on other investments exceeds the total rate of return on community bank and bank holding company securities? Many shareholders remain loyal—not because they expect the highest rate of return on their securities but because they support the community institution and are willing to accept a lower rate of return.

However, shareholder loyalty can change—and does. If your banking institution receives an offer of three times book value, most shareholders will decide to sell. Nurture shareholders through consistent communications, honesty, and a genuine effort to meet their demands and conditions. Shareholder loyalty is difficult to destroy at most community banking institutions in this country—but it can happen by ignoring their importance to the survival of the financial institution. Develop programs to ensure that shareholders remain loyal.

Key 3: What Shareholders Do Not Know Can Harm the Institution

The board of directors regularly deals with unfortunate financial performance, bad loan quality, or capital inadequacy. An unbelievable number of boards attempt to solve these problems (often aided by senior management) without informing the shareholders of the problem. Senior management and the board of directors believe that if shareholders discovered these difficulties, there could be repercussions. That is absolutely correct! However, the best way to solve the problem is not to hush it up. If shareholders find out about adverse financial performance or conditions in the banking institution through the grapevine, rumor, innuendo, or, worse, through local newspaper, radio, or television, the problem could be blown out of proportion. Avoid potential problems. Come clean and issue a carefully worded, full disclosure directed to the shareholders.

Shareholder response to adverse news regarding their bank or thrift has too often been to file suit against the board of directors and senior management. It is increasingly common that your list of shareholders may include a professional litigator who will not hesitate to push for a cash settlement. When financial performance and/or conditions are concealed, the board is in jeopardy of receiving charges of misrepresentation, fraud, and dereliction of duty. To protect the bank or thrift against possible litigations, inform shareholders of any adverse financial conditions, substandard lending performance, or administrative orders.

Key 4: Organizing the Shareholders Communications Function

Appropriate shareholder relations and communications is the responsibility of the board of directors. The board of directors can delegate some of this responsibility to senior management by utilizing an ad hoc committee or making it part of the executive committee duties and responsibilities. Shareholder relations should be a significant consideration at all board and appropriate committee meetings at all times. Review the quality of shareholder relations and communications on a quarterly basis. Annually evaluate shareholder relations and communications goals, objectives, and performance. Implement any required modifications as quickly as possible.

Key 5: The Shareholder Relations and Communications Officer

Senior management should appoint a shareholder relations and communications officer. The person who holds this position is responsible for implementation of the shareholder relations and communications program. Although this officer may also not be selected as the bank or thrift's official spokesperson, he or she is responsible for the dissemination of all financial as well as ancillary information that is disclosed to the public. This includes handling the annual shareholders' meeting, special shareholders' meetings, and mass media shareholder communications. The shareholder relations and communications officer should report directly to senior management and through them is accountable to the board.

Key 6: Shareholder Relations Task Force

Every banking organization should have an emergency task force for shareholder relations and communications. Today's banking environment changes quickly, making a financial institution susceptible at any time to an unsolicited merger or acquisition. A very practical reason for an emergency task force is so that major shareholders can be contacted immediately and responses to hostile takeovers can be developed. Planning by the task force eliminates panic when emergency situations occur, allowing an organization to act efficiently.

Not all emergencies are hostile takeover attempts. False or negative publicity disseminated by the media could cause depository and / or lending problems. Such a situation would require action by the emergency task force to counteract any derogatory information. Even accurate disclosure of grim financial statements, loan loss problems, capital inadequacies or management ethical problems may prompt the emergency task force to take remedial actions quickly.

Key 7: Development of Bank Spokesperson

Separate from the shareholder relations and communications officer, each banking institution needs someone to speak on behalf of the bank or thrift and handle communications with the press. It is quite probable (but not required) that the spokesperson is the same person designated as the shareholder relations and communications officer. The spokesperson should be available at all times for communications with the media. She or he should be able to develop rapport and credibility with the press and shareholders. The spokesperson should answer questions fully, be factually accurate, and never duck hard questions. If unable to respond correctly to a question, he or she should find the answer. This individual should be the epitome of creditability and ethical standards for the banking institution. Accordingly, involve the spokesperson in appropriate meetings of the board of directors and senior management so that he or she receives accurate information to disseminate information to the media.

Key 8: Shareholder Relations at a Problem Bank

If the bank or thrift should find itself on the problem bank list, the situation could worsen if shareholder relations and communications are not handled properly. A simple fork in the road could become an inescapable maze if not corrected immediately.

The easiest rule to follow is to tell the truth! Deviations from the truth will create bigger problems with shareholders and the media. Tell the truth promptly, and continue to do so. If asked sensitive questions, give appropriate answers.

Make sure shareholders receive unfavorable information (by phone if necessary) before the press. Information leaks happen even in the best organizations. Rumors that are circulated around the banking community come from within organizations, not the press. Disclosure of problems and plans for solutions renews creditability of the banking institution with shareholders. Depositors and borrowers will show their appreciation for full disclosure and even insist that the problem is handled with courtesy and goodwill by the press.

Key 9: Communicate Objectives to Shareholders and the Public

As a rule, community banking institutions do not share information regarding the future direction of the institution with their shareholders. One advantage of solid shareholder relations and communications is that goals and objectives can be delivered to shareholders and the public in a fashion and schedule as desired by the board and management. After the board of directors adopts the corporate mission and the strategic plan for the next several years, distribute a summarized strategic plan (eliminating proprietary goals and objectives from public disclosure) to shareholders and the public. The corporate mission, likewise, should be disseminated in order to obtain the most favorable publicity possible. This is positive shareholder relations and communications and should be used to its fullest advantage.

Distribute financial information on a regular basis (quarterly, semiannually, and yearly) concerning how well the bank or thrift is doing and where it hopes to be in years to come. If not constrained by SEC reporting rules and regulations, a little more freedom may be gained when projecting future performance. To favorably influence shareholder loyalty, public creditability, and (needless to say) stock price, disseminate appropriate significant aspects over and above legally required disclosures.

There are many types of items that can be disclosed to improve shareholder relations and communications. These include: (1) significant officer changes; (2) promotions and changes in staff; (3) financial performance; (4) mergers and acquisitions; (5) building facilities, including head offices and / or branches; (6) ATM expansion improvements; and (7) important community activities. Controlled disclosure of information by the shareholder relations and communications officer of information is much more preferable to reacting to adverse situations.

Key 10: Shareholder Relations and Communications—A Two-Way Street

The shareholders relations campaign should be a two-way street. On a regular basis, solicit shareholders' comments about their investment, their needs, and their desires as shareholders of the banking institution. Determine whether they are in favor of the actions taken by the board of directors and senior management. Find out if their investment return is satisfactory in relation to other competitive and alternative instruments.

A program established for contacting and communicating with shareholders provides a useful feedback mechanism. Utilize business reply envelopes, survey questionnaires directed to shareholders, focus groups, and personal contacts with significant shareholders to develop an appropriate feedback mechanism. If a majority of shareholders are located within the community, personal contact and focus groups are far more appropriate than telephone surveys, and questionnaires are far better than no feedback at all. Personal contacts of board members and senior management with significant shareholders to determine their likes and dislikes are essential, regardless of whether shareholders are local or national in nature. Contacting shareholders on a regular basis cultivates their support. Include shareholders in activities of the financial institution. Invite significant shareholders into the bank on a regular quarterly or semiannual basis to highlight favorable (and even not so favorable) events, answer their questions, and provide personal and direct face-to-face contact and attention. Invite local shareholders to special bank sponsored programs. The list of topics is endless, including discussions regarding national and local economic conditions, new products and services, tax ramifications of current legislation, estate planning, financial planning, and so on.

Key 11: The Media and Relations and Communications

It is of immeasurable importance for improving shareholder and public communications to cultivate a friendly relationship with the mass media, including local regional and/or national print, radio and TV journalists. These individuals are professionals whose goals are to report what they believe is newsworthy, with or without your cooperation. Without cooperation, your side of the story may never be told or may be reported inaccurately. Treat the media with respect, candor, full cooperation, and always provide the truth. Never underestimate the persistence, sagacity, and intelligence of the media.

Develop a program of regular contacts with media personnel. Invite them to the bank on a regular basis to discuss current events at the banking institution. Arrange public interviews and personal contacts with senior management and board members with the press to answer follow-up questions concerning the management and operations of the institution. Whenever interviews occur, contact local shareholders so that they know ahead of time. Consider sending shareholders the text or excerpts of public interviews and or discussions of management's performance.

The most inappropriate behavior a banking institution can exhibit is to threaten the press with reprisals for printing or broadcasting reports that do not portray the best side of the bank or thrift. First of all, such threats do not work. Second, the press will continue to issue disparaging reports, and any contact or rapport with the press is lost. Furthermore, if the media reports something you don't like, consider carefully whether the report was inaccurate, or whether the action was wrong. It is possible that the media is correct. Know area journalists and know their strengths as well as their weaknesses. They are human beings (although it may not always be obvious) with faults like anyone else. Cultivate their attention and respect, and treat them as well as any other customer of the bank or thrift. Attempt to improve positive reports of the bank or thrift's activities and those of competitors and colleagues in the financial institution field. Remember, the media have wider reporting networks than any disgruntled customer will ever have and can do more damage in one column than word of mouth can achieve in months.

Make educating the press on financial and banking traditions, performances, and trends a major positive effort. Providing factual information in these areas allows the media to create comprehensive and understandable reports. Make sure that your organization is a source to which they can turn for honest information. Cooperation will result in improving understanding and more favorable treatment of the bank or thrift.

Finally, follow three rules when dealing with the press: (1) Never lie; (2) always be available, even if it takes extra effort; and (3) answer all questions or find out the answers to questions and report back to the press. In the long run, these three maxims will help develop an excellent communications program with the mass media.

Key 12: Control the Shareholders List

If the goal of the banking institution is to survive—control the shareholders list. Many of today's securities are listed in street or nominee names which makes it difficult to identify the actual shareholders. The secretary of the corporation is responsible for patrolling the shareholders list on a routine basis. Track down purchases made in street names or nominees to discover the true owners. Remember that in all likelihood, these individuals will never receive direct financial statements. They will be buried somewhere in a brokerage firm in New York. Every member of the board of directors and senior management should have a list of shareholders at their disposal. Divide the list into segments so that every director and senior manager can quickly contact major shareholders in case of emergencies. Be very careful that these lists do not fall into unfriendly hands.

The list of shareholders should be consistently analyzed for age, location, and status. Shareholders continue to age. As this occurs, they may wish to liquidate their investments. Develop procedures to control the shareholders list through corporate stock redemption, active local securities markets, and other techniques that shareholders can use to resell securities without actually offering their stock on the open market (or worse, becoming attracted by an offer to sell to another organization). Beneficiaries of deceased shareholders are usually not very loyal, they often do not live in the area, and they really prefer cash. Controlling the shareholder list is essential to survival.

Key 13: The Annual Shareholders Meeting

In many cases, the annual shareholders meeting is a wasted opportunity. Even the best chair and president gets nervous when it is time to show up and talk to shareholders. Instead of trying to strut their stuff and highlight the bank or thrift's performance in a fancy "dog and pony show" fashion, this meeting should emphasize the quality of management and staff, entertain shareholders, and deliver valuable information to develop stronger shareholder relations. Too many annual shareholders meetings are perfunctory, held at inopportune times, bulldozed through in 15 minutes, and attended only by those who have nothing else to do. What a wasted opportunity! The shareholders meeting is the most important shareholders relations tool.

Develop a program for the shareholders meetings that is the envy of social meetings in the community. Many community banks and thrifts are located in communities or suburbs where this annual meeting can be the social highlight of the year. The worst possible decision is to hold the meeting in the lobby at 3:00 p.m. on Wednesday afternoon when the bank or thrift is closed. That is not the best time to encourage shareholder attendance. It may work for those who are retired, but many other shareholders probably are making a living at that time of day. The shareholders meeting should be an evening meeting (or even a Saturday morning meeting). Serve refreshments and dinner. Make it really special for shareholders, they're worth the effort. Some may complain that such a program cuts into their dividends, but the majority will appreciate the attention.

If the annual shareholders' meeting is one to be remembered, people will not want to miss it the following year. This is the time to deliver the best shareholder relations posture and to impress shareholders with the bank's abilities, performance, and opportunities. The shareholder relations and communications officer should be responsible for making this one of the highlights of the bank year and should be allowed to spend the necessary funds to attract shareholders year in and year out.

Key 14: Shareholder Communications

Truly personal-oriented banking institutions communicate with their shareholders. The shareholder relations and communications officer operates under a regular and planned communications program with shareholders. Semiannually or quarterly, dividend notices include a personal communications piece to each shareholder. With today's word processing programs, each piece can be personalized without extreme extra cost. An effective shareholder communications program simply requires a well-defined plan and lots of coordination to accomplish.

As a minimum, shareholders should be communicated with quarterly—when dividend statements and quarterly financial statements are sent. However, send out more than just an abbreviated financial statement. Send all statements, since under the Freedom of Information Act they are public information. Communicate with shareholders whenever anything is relevant or important to their knowledge. These opportunities can also be used to explain recent events, reasons for less than adequate performance, or even explanations that the bank is healthy and expanding on future projections. Shareholders should receive any significant information that will benefit them and improve shareholder relations.

Key 15: Shareholders Should Be the First to Know

The shareholder relations and communications program is geared to one premise—that shareholders should receive information from you rather than the media. If the bank or thrift has decided to sell, or developed a new product or service, as often as possible, shareholders should know before the press reports the event or conditions. If possible, press releases should be sent to shareholders before being sent to the media. If the press does pick up on information before shareholders, make sure materials are sent to shareholders immediately. It is amazing how many organizations do not keep a supply of printed mailing labels for their own shareholder base. Shareholders deserve to be the first to know.

SUMMARY

Understanding the value of shareholder relations and communications is an important part of the strategic plan and can assist in maintaining shareholder loyalty and satisfaction with current and future operations, and project an attitude of competency and creditability. Work toward shareholder loyalty, mass media acceptance, and developing an excellent reputation as a community banking institution. These do not happen simply because the bank or thrift operates on a sound and profitable basis. It is important to control the situation. A controlled and positive shareholder relations and communications program is necessary to achieve the goals of a community banking institution.

BIBLIOGRAPHY

"Auditing Your Bank's Strategic Plan." *Bank Directors Report* 15, Issue 9 (March 1984): 5.

"Bank Executives Face Enormous Strategic Challenges." *American Bankers Weekly* 8 (August 1989): 2.

"Bank Links Research to Strategic Planning." *Bank Advertising News* 11 (April 1987): 11.

"Cost Cutting and Restructuring for Profitability: Strategic Implications for Banks." *Bank Operations Report (Part 1)* 18 (September 1988): 1–2.

"Developing a Technology Strategy for Your Bank." *Bank Operations Report (Part 2)* 18 (February 1989): 4–5.

"Financial Institutions Need to Upgrade Strategic Management." *Savings Institutions* 105 (July 1984): 147–148.

"Getting Outside Help: The Pros and Cons." *Bank Management* (March/April 1994): 67.

"Helping Banks Plan for Electronic Banking." *Bank Operations Report* 13 (February 1984): 4–6.

"How Strategic Planning Turned a Bank Around (Western State Bank, St. Paul, Minneapolis)." *American Banking Association Banking Journal* 78 (June 1986): 6.

"One Strategy Doesn't Fit All." *ABA Banking Journal* 85 (September 1993): 72–74

"Providing a Business Plan." *National Thrift News* 9 (September 1985): 29.

"Rumors of the Demise of Strategic Planning Are Greatly Exaggerated Consultant Concludes: Bankers More Than Others Appreciate the Discipline." *Financial Services Strategy* (May 1985): 5–6.

"Strategic Planning," *Bank Auditing and Accounting Report* 17 (October 1984): 5–6.

"Strategic Planning Gets High Marks from Bank CEOs." *Bank Executives Report* 21 (June 1985): 5–6.

"Strategic Planning Gets High Marks from Bank CEOs; Increasing Focus Is on Implementation Says Study." *Bank Operations Report* (May 1985): 8.

"Strategic Planning for Regulatory Change Is Key to Community Bank Performance and Survival." *Bank Directors Report* 15 (April 1984): 6.

"Strategic Planning: How Lagging Banks Can Get Started." *Bank Executives Report* 20 (April 1984): 3–4.

"Strategic Planning in Banks: It's Not a Cure-All Says Study." *Bank Personnel Report* 19 (August 1986): 6–7.

"Strategic Planning: The Four S's." *Western Banker* 77 (August 1985): 23.

"Strategic Planning Will Produce Long-Range Benefits to Bank." *Mid-Continent Banker* 81 (April 1985): 4.

"What's Ahead in Technology . . . Blind Spot in Strategic Planning?" *Management Review* 73 (October 1984): 26–28+.

Allaire, Y., and M. Firsiratu. "Coping with Strategic Uncertainty." *Sloan Management Review* 30 (Spring 1989): 7–16.

Alworth, "Mid-Sized Banks Frustrated as They Try Strategic Planning." *Bank Marketing* 21 (October 1989): 36–37.

Aspinwall, Richard C., and Eisenbeis, R. A. *Handbook for Banking Strategy*. New York: Wiley, 1985.

Austin, Douglas V. "A Guide to Short-term Strategic Planning." *Bankers Magazine* 166 (November/December 1983): 22–28.

Austin, Douglas V., et al. *Capital Planning for the Community Bank*. Rolling Meadows, Ill.: Bank Administration Institute, 1988.

Austin, Douglas, V. *Inside the Board Room: How to Be an Effective Bank Director*. Homewood, Ill.: Dow Jones-Irwin, 1989.

Austin, Douglas V. "The Strategic Plan." *Northwestern Financial Review* 174 (September 1989): 20

Austin, Douglas V., et al. *Modern Banking*. 2d ed. Rolling Meadows, Ill.: Bank Administration Institute, 1988.

Austin, Douglas V. "Practical Planning Suggestions for Community Banks." *Bankers Magazine* 173 (July/August 1990): 78–82

Austin, Douglas V. "Why Strategic Plan? Why Survive?" *CBAI Illinois Banknotes* (April/May 1992): 8.

Austin, Douglas V. "Your Bank's Strategic Plan: Now That You Have One, What Can You Do with It." *Independent Banker* (November 1995): 25–28.

Austin, Douglas V., and Mandula, Mark S. *Banker's Handbook for Strategic Planning.* Boston, Mass.: Bankers Publishing Company, 1985.

Austin, Douglas V., and Mandula, M. "Situation Analysis: A First Step in Strategic Planning." *Mid-Continent Banker* 81 (April 1985): BG-10+.

Austin, Douglas V., and Scampini, T. "Long-Term Strategic Planning." *Bankers Magazine* 167 (January / February 1984): 61–66.

Austin, Douglas V., and Simoff, Paul L. *Strategic Planning for Banks: Meeting the Challenges of the 1990s.* Rolling Meadows, Ill.: Bankers Publishing Company, 1990.

Beachman, J. "Prescription for Community Banks: Strategy, Strategy, Strategy, Strategy." *Bank Administration* 50 (June 1989): 8+.

Bennet, T. "Bankers Should Know What They Want before Calling in Planning Consultants." *American Banker* 149 (June 1984): 14.

Bennet, T., and Overby T. "Putting Change to Work: A Checklist of Performance Objectives." *Independent Banker* 36 (September 1986): 54–57.

Bettinger, C. "Behind the Mission Statement." *ABA Banking Journal* 77 (October 1985): 154+.

Bettinger, C. *High Performance in the 90s: Leading the Strategic and Cultural Revolution in Banking.* Homewood, Ill.: Business One Irwin, 1990.

Bettinger, C. "Strategic Planning, Marketing Strategy, and Shareholder Value." *Hoosier Banker* (September 1993): 12–16.

Bexley, J. B. "Director Involvement in the Strategic Plan." *Bank Administration* 61 (August 1985): 32–33.

Beynon, W. D., and Howes, M. E. "Your Bank's Business Strategy: A Prerequisite for Merging Successfully." *Bank Administration* 63 (August 1987): 22+.

Bird, Anat. "A 1990s Twist on Strategic Planning." *Bankers Magazine* 174 (March / April 1991): 66–69.

Bird, Anat. "Strategic Coping—the Planning Process at Troubled Banks." *Bankers Magazine* 175 (July / August 1992): 57–62.

Bonelli, R. A. "Corporate Planning a Growing Role among the Regionals." *Bankers Magazine* 170 (July / August 1987): 43–48.

Brown, Albert J. *High Performance Banking: How to Improve Earnings in Any Bank.* Rolling Meadows, Ill.: Bankers Publishing Company, 1990.

Cady, Joseph H. "How Does Your Strategic Plan Really Rate?" *ABA Banking Journal* (October 1994): 106.

Castorina, S. A. "Strategic Systems Planning in the Community Bank." *Bank Administration* 64 (Fall 1988): 9.

Chorafas, Dimitris N. *Information Systems in Financial Institutions: A Guide to Strategic Planning, based on the Japanese Experience.* Englewood Cliffs, N.J.: Prentice-Hall, 1983.

Chorafas, Dimitris N. *Strategic Planning for Electronic Banking: From Human Resources to Product Development and Information Systems.* St. Paul, Minn.: Butterworths, 1987.

Cramer, Robert H., et al. *Strategic Planning Manual: A Compliance Guide.* Madison, Wisconsin: MemberServ, 1990.

Day, George S. "Strategies for Surviving a Shakeout." *Harvard Business Review* 75 (March 1997) 92–102.

Deshpande A., and Parasuraman A. "Linking Corporate Culture to Strategic Planning." *Business Horizons* 29 (May / June 1986): 28–37.

Deutsch, B. "Using the Strategic Planning Retreat Profitably." *American Banker* 153 (July 1988): 4+.

Donaldson, G. "Financial Goals & Strategic Consequences." *Harvard Business Review* 63 (May / June 1985): 57–66.

Donnelly, James H. *The New Banker: Developing Leadership in a Dynamic Era.* Homewood, Ill.: Dow Jones-Irwin, 1989.

Dunn, P. "Strategic Planning for Bank Card Organizations." *Southern Banker* 166 (November 1986): 32+.

Dyche, D. "1985 A Time to Revisit the Strategic Plan." *Bankers Magazine* 168 (March / April 1985): 39–43.

Earle, Dennis M. "The Critical Mesh in Strategic Planning." *Bankers Magazine* 174 (May / June 1991): 48–53.

Emerson, E. "Strategic Plan Development Must Include Work Force." *American Banker* 153 (February 1988): 4.

Fabian, J. "Strategic Planning Ever More Important to Assure ATM / POS Usage Profitability." *Mid-Continent Banker* 81 (March 1985): 7–8.

Ferguson, W. "A Business Plan in Your Future? Here Are Some Steps to Do It Right." *Bottomline* 3 (August 1986): 35–37.

Fish, "Strategic Planning—You Can and Must Get Started!" *Oklahoma Bankers* 47 (August 1988): 16–17.

Fitzgerald, T. "The Banker, the Entrepreneur and the Planning Connection." *Bottomline* 4 (December 1987): 49–50+.

Foster, W. "Planning for Sales Success." *Mid-Continent Banker* 82 (August 1986): 18–19+.

Fraust, B. "A Strategic Planning Blueprint Can Fortify the Smaller Bank." *American Banker* 149 (June 11, 1984): 24.

Frazer, D., and Kolari, J. "A Bright Future for Community Banks." *Independent Banker* 37 (January 1987): 38–41+.

Furash, E. "To Maximize Bank's Value, Pay Attention to the Basics." *Financial Services Strategy* 14 (April 1985): 1+.

Gaudet, B. "Integrated Data Systems Support Strategic Planning." *Savings Institutions* 106 (September 1985): 546–550.

Giesen, D. "Prudent Business Planning Sidesteps Risk Pitfalls." *Savings Institution* 107 (1986): 58–65+.

Gray, D. "Uses and Misuses of Strategic Planning." *Harvard Business Review* 136 (April 1986): 36–37+.

Gunderson, L. "Planning for Survival . . . Differentiation as a Competitive Tool." *Oklahoma Banker* 45 (December 1986): 17–18+.

Guttman, Robert. *Reforming Money and Finance: Institutions & Markets in Flux*. Armonk, N.Y.: M. E. Sharpe, 1989.

Gup, B. E., and Whitehead, D. "Strategic Planning in Banks—Does It Pay?" *Long Range Planning* 22 (Fall 1989): 124–130.

Gup, W. "Bank Strategy in an Age of Rapid Change." *The Banker* 136 (April 1986): 36–37+.

Haas, P., and Wemple, W. W. "Planning for Change in Banking: Be Prepared." *Bank Magazine* 169 (November / December 1986): 55–59.

Hadler, P. A. "Few Words to the Wise for Some Thrifts Eyeing Increased Size." *American Banker* 153 (January 1988): 4+.

Hagopian, J. "Long Range Planning: It's Your Bank's Future." *Independent Banker* 36 (December 1986): 10–20+.

Haley, S. "The Changing Financial Environment: Planning and Implementing Well." *Western Banker* 77 (September 1985): 11.

Hamel, G., and Prahglard, C. "Strategic Intent: To Revitalize Corporate Performance, We Need a Whole New Model of Strategy." *Harvard Business* 67 (May / June 1989): 63–76.

Hammermesh, R. "Making Planning Strategic." *Harvard Business Review* 64 (July / August 1986): 115–120.

Harold, Geoffrey. *Strategic Systems Planning for Financial Institutions: Using Automated Solutions and Technology for Competitive Advantages.* Chicago, Ill.: Probus Publishing, 1993.

Hart, Berne. "Strategic Planning Responsibility of the CEO." *Bank Management* (March 1984): 79.

Hayes, R. "Strategic Planning—Forward in Reverse?" *Harvard Business Review* 63 (November / December 1985): 111–119.

Heckman, R. "Strategic Planning for Information Technology." *Bankers Magazine* 171 (September / October 1988): 68–72.

Heikus, D. J., and Raymond J. "Productivity: Strategic Imperative for Banks." *Bank Administration* 61 (December 1985): 38+.

Higgins, Michael T. "Planning for Banking's Future: An Exciting & Manageable Task." *Banking News* 84 (December 1985): 38.

Higgins, Michael T. *Beyond Survival: How Financial Institutions Can Survive in the 1990s.* Homewood, Ill.: Dow Jones-Irwin, 1990.

Isenberg, D. "The Tactics of Strategic Opportunities." *Harvard Business Review* 65 (March / April 1987): 92–97.

Jackson, C. "Training's Role in the Process of Planned Change." *Training & Development Journal* 39 (February 1985): 70–74.

James, B. "Strategic Planning under Fire." *Sloan Management Review* 25 (Summer 1984): 57–62.

Jannott, Paul E. *The Effective Bank Supervisor: How to Develop Management Skills.* Boston: Bankers Publishing Company, 1985.

Jewell, D. et al. "For the First-Time Planner." *Supervisory Management* 29 (July 1984): 40–42.

Jewett, W. et al. "Restructuring under New Capital Regulations: Asking the Right Questions." *Bankers Magazine* 172 (March/April 1989): 9–14.

Johnson, T. "Assessing Risks & Profitability in the U.S. Banking System." *Journal of Commercial Bank Lending* 70 (October 1987): 41–47.

Kargar, Javad. "Successful Implementation of Strategic Decisions in Small Community Banks." *Journal of Small Business Management* 32 (April 1994): 10–22.

Kaufman, G. G., and Kornendi, R. C. *Deregulating Financial Services: Public Policy in Flux.* Cambridge, Mass.: Bellinger Publishing Company, 1980.

Kaufman, R. "A Needs Assessment Primer." *Training & Development Journal* 41 (October 1987): 78–83.

Kauss, J. "A Guide to Strategic Planning for Banks." *Bank Administration* 63 (August 1987): 18–19.

Keane, J. "Focusing on the Corporate Future: Not a Trivial Pursuit." *Business Horizons* 30 (January/February 1987): 25–33.

Keefe, L. "Community Bankers Learn from Good, Bad Experiences." *ABA Bankers Weekly* 8 (January 1989): 8.

Kerr, D., and Wilson, R. "Banks Must See Need to Focus on Care Business." *American Banker* 152 (June 1987): 4+.

Killebrew, R. "Road Map to Growth Lies in Planning." *Bank Marketing* 19 (October 1987): 31.

Layton, S. L. "To Outsmart the Competition, Try a Little Strategic Planning." *Bank Marketing* 19 (November 1987): 7.

Leemputte, P. "Strategic Repositioning for Shareholder Value." *Issues in Bank Regulation* 12 (Spring 1989): 7–10.

Lemke, L. "Mission Statements Must Encourage Performance." *Bank Marketing* 19 (July 1987): 43.

Lenz, R. "Managing the Evolution of the Strategic Planning Process." *Business Horizons* 30 (January/February 1987): 34–39.

Levine, M., and Clause J. "Developing a Crisis Management." *Bankers Magazine* 169 (January/February 1986): 35–39.

Linkow, P. "At the Roots of Corporate Strategy." *Training and Development Journal* 39 (May 1985): 85–87.

Litan, Robert E. *What Should Banks Do?* Washington, D.C.: Brookings Institute, 1987.

Little, M. "The Key to Profitability at Small Business Clients: The Business Plan." *Journal of Commercial Bank Lending* 70 (August 1988): 34–38.

Luke, R. "Arizona Bank Expects Cost Cutting to Bear Fruit Despite Resistance." *American Banker* 153 (May 1988): 24+.

Lutes, T. "A Blueprint for Asset/Liability Management." *Bank Accounting and Finance* 2 (Fall 1988): 27–30.

Lyles, G. "Strategic Planning That Works." *Bottomline* (June 1987): 61+.

Mascenzi, R. "How to Develop a Strategic Marketing Plan." *Bank Marketing* 16 (October 1984): 26–29.

Matthews, G., and Menstadt, D. "Restructuring Seen as Key to Bank Survival." *American Banker* 152 (October 1987): 1+.

McClure, S., and Lamping, M. "The Benefits of Strategic Planning in a Changing Environment." *Ohio Banker* 77 (February 1985): 20–24.

McConkey, D. "Planning in a Changing Environment." *Business Horizons* 31 (September/October 1988): 64–72.

McQuistion, Dennis. "Your Board: To Plan, or Not to Plan . . . This Is *not* the Issue." *Kentucky Bankers Magazine* (April 1994): 8–11.

Metviner, N. "Putting Quality to Work in Banking." *Bankers Magazine* 171 (September/October 1988): 47–52.

Metzger, R. "Challenging the Strategic Assumptions at the Banking Industry." *Bankers Magazine* 167 (July/August 1984): 29–34.

Metzger, R. "Strategic Marketing for Banks." *Consumer Banking Digest* 5 (September 1985): 10–11.

Metzger, R. "Banks: True to Their Mission." *Bankers Monthly* 104 (September 1987): 14.

Miller, Richard B. *Super Banking: Innovative Management Strategies (that work).* Homewood, Ill.: Dow Jones-Irwin, 1989.

Miller, W. "Increased Productivity—the Banker's Goal in Long-Range Planning." *Mid-Continent Banker* 81 (April 1985): BG6–BG9.

Miller, W. "Master Plan: Capitalizing on Opportunity: Is Implementation the Weak Link?" *Texas Banking* 76 (February 1986): 20+.

Miller, W. "Strategic Planning: Wasted if not Implemented." *Hoosier Banker* 71 (February 1987): 10+.

Mitzberg, H. "Crafting Strategy." *Harvard Business Review* 65 (July / August 1987) 66–75.

Mitzberg, H. "The Strategy Concept II: Another Look at Why Organizations Need Strategies." *California Management Review* 30 (Fall 1987): 25–32.

Mitzberg, H. "The Strategy Concept II: Five Ps for Strategy." *California Management Review* 30 (Fall 1987): 11–24.

Molard, R. "The Business of Planning." *Credit Union Management* (July 1988): 18–20+.

Moran, J. "Strategic Planning Made Easier." *Hoosier Banker* 69 (September 1985): 30–31.

Moran, M. "In Aftermath of Deregulation Be Selective in Strategic Choices." *Financial Services Strategy* 1 (August 1985): I+.

Morrall, Katherine. "Piecing Together a Strategic Plan (Corporate planning for banks)." *Bank Marketing* (September 1996): 26.

Morrisy G. "Who Needs a Mission Statement? You Do." *Training & Development Journal* 42 (March 1988): 50–52.

Morton, M., and Corbett, T. "Market Repositioning: The Challenge for Medium-Sized Banks." *Bankers Magazine* 167 (May / June 1984): 60–65.

Mudler, Paul S., and Miller, Richard B. *The Banking Jungle: How to Survive & Prosper in a Business Turned Topsy Turvy.* New York: Wiley, 1989.

Murray, W. "Coordinating Strategic Planning with Asset/Liability Management." *Bank/Asset Liability Management* 4 (August 1988): 4–5.

Nichols, Grove. "Strategic Plans That Work Are a Must (Part 1)." *ABA Banking Journal* 88 (June 1996): 20–24.

Norris, E. "Strategic Planner Steers Decisions: Listening to the Market Place Is the Route to Customer Relationships." *Savings Institutions* 109 (September 1988): S42–43.

Odiorne, G. "For Successful Succession Planning . . . Match Organizational Requirements to Corporate Human Potential." *Management Review* 73 (November 1984): 49–51.

Patin, S. "Strategic Planning: A Blueprint for Growth." *Independent Banker* 35 (September 1985): 20–23.

Pearson, D. "Long-Range Planning Is Key to Automated Platform Strategy." *Bank Systems and Equipment* 21 (February 1984): 140.

Petrick, C. "Business Planning as a Tool for Managing Risk." *Federal Home Loan Bank of Seattle: Bank News* (Summer 1987): 11–15.

Poelker, J. "Developing a Comprehensive Financial Framework for Business Planning." *Bank Administration* 64 (December 1988): 44+.

Pope, M. "When You Set Goals Be Sure of Your Capacity to Attain Them." *American Banker* (October 1986): 4+.

Pope, M. "Invite All of the Troops to Help Map Out the Plan of Attack." *American Banker* 149 (October 1989): 4+.

Poquette, B. "The Retail Force and Corporate Culture: Two Studies Chart Banking's Future Course." *Bank News* 85 (July 1986): 9+.

Price, J. "New Business Directions Demand Smarter Staffing Strategies." *Savings Institutions* 109 (June 1988): 62–66.

Price, J. "Entrepreneurial Planning: Quick-Start Strategic Planning Stresses Action and Promotes Changes." *Savings Institutions* 109 (August 1988): 74–78.

Rau, S. "Shakeout Strategies for Banks." *ABA Banking Journal* 76 (September 1984): 126+.

Rau, S. "Why Planning Ain't What It Used to Be." *Bankers Magazine* 171 (May/June 1988): 66–70.

Rau, S. "Managing Diversity: Banking's Next Strategic Challenge." *Bankers Magazine* 171 (May/June 1988): 66–70.

Raudsepp, D. "Establishing a Creative Climate: Two Dozen Ways to Turn on Your Organization's Light Bulb." *Training & Development Journal* 41 (April 1987): 50–53.

Raymond, M., and Barksdale, H. "Corporate Strategic Planning & Corporate Marketing: Toward an Interface?" *Business Horizons* 32 (September/October 1989): 41–48.

Rich, S., and Gumpert, D. "How to Write a Winning Business Plan." *Harvard Business Review* 63 (May/June 1985): 156–621+.

Richardson, Linda. *Winning Negotiation Strategies for Bankers.* Homewood, Ill.: Dow Jones-Irwin, 1987.

Rizzi, J. "Restructuring Opportunities for Commercial Banks." *Bankers Magazine* 172 (May/June 1989): 73–77.

Rohlwink, Anthony. *Strategic Positioning for Financial Institutions: A Planner for Achieving Competitive Advantage in the International Market Place.* London; New York: Woodhead-Faulkner, 1991.

Rose, Peter S. *The Changing Structure of American Banking.* New York: Columbia University Press, 1987.

Rosenberg, L., and Schewe, C. "Strategic Planning: Fulfilling the Promise." *Business Horizons* 11 (July/August 1985): 54–62.

Roussakis, Emmanuel, N. *Commercial Banking in an Era of Deregulation.* New York: Praeger, 1984.

Salem, G. "Ten Ideas to Help You Cope, Adapt & Prosper." *ABA Banking Journal* 76 (February 1984): 28.

Sapp, Richard W. "Strategic Management for Bankers." Oxford, Ohio: Planning Executives Institute, 1984.

Savona, Paolo, and Sutija, George (eds). *Strategic Planning in International Banking.* New York: St. Martin's Press, 1986.

Schifrin, Matthew. "Merrillizing the World." *Forbes* 159 (February 1997): 146–151.

Schilit, K. "How to Write a Winning Business Plan." *Business Horizons* 30 (September / October 1987): 13–22.

Schreck, R. "Dust Off That Plan." *ABA Banking Journal* 79 (October 1987): 140.

Scott, G. "Sound Strategic Planning for the Medium-Sized Bank." *Bankers Magazine* 169 (March / April 1986): 26–31.

Shin, "Strategic Positioning in Operations Management." *Bankers Magazine* 168 (March / April 1985): 11–14.

Shostack, G. "Gamesmanship in Planning May Lead to Impossible Hurdles." *American Banker* 149 (September 1989): 4+.

Simonson, Donald G. "Planning Holds Key to Consolidation." *US Banker* 105 (August 1995): 72–73.

Silverman, M., and Greene, J. "Strategic Direction in Community Banking." *Journal of Retail Banking* (Fall 1988): 41–51.

Sisk, R. "Strategic Planning—Get Hopping." *Independent Banker* 38 (August 1988): 10–12.

Slaughter, S. "Strategic Planning: Marketing's Foundation." *Independent Banker* 3 (March 1987): 26–27.

Slostack, G. "Designing Services That Deliver." *Harvard Business Review* (January / February 1984): 133–139.

Smith, R., and Sapp, R. "Exercising Strategic Muscle: Linking Budgets to Strategy." *Texas Banker* 3 (November 1989): 16+.

Soat, J. "Mastering the Art of Strategic Planning through Simulation." *Office Administration and Automation* 45 (November 1984): 28–30+.

Soukup, William R. "Strategic Planning Is Not Long-Term Budgeting." *ABA Banking Journal* 84 (November 1992): 20.

Spence, Franklin F. "Embrace the Future with an Effective Strategic Plan." *Bank Management* (March / April 1994): 64.

Spooner, L. "Savers Survey Sets the Stage for Strategic Planning." *Savings Institutions* 60 (May 1985): 72–79.

Stedman, M. "The Strategy of Strategic Communications: Aimless Public Relations Efforts Are a Ticket to Disaster. Strategic Planning Can Avoid the Pitfalls Many Banks Have Stumbled Upon." *Bankers Monthly* 106 (October 1989): 87.

Stewart, B., and Glassman, D. "Why Restructuring Adds Value: Leveraging to a Bigger Carrot." *Cash Flow* 9 (January 1988): 36+.

Stewart, B., and Glassman, D. "Why Restructuring Adds Value: When Subtracting Is a Plus." *Cash Flow* 9 (February 1988): 46–48.

Sullivan, C. "Reasoning by Analogy—A Tool for Business Planning." *Sloan Management Review* 29 (Spring 1988): 55–60.

Sullivan, M. "Banks Must Decide Whether to Change—or Die." *American Banker* 153 (April 1988): 4.

Taylor, Bernard, and de Maubray, Guy (eds.). *Strategic Planning for Financial Institutions.* London: Bodley Head & HFL, 1974.

Terracciano, A. "Setting the Restructuring Agenda (interview)." *Bankers Magazine* 172 (March/April 1989): 5–8.

Thamara, T. *Bankers Guide to New Growth Opportunities.* Englewood Cliffs, N. J.: Prentice Hall, 1988.

Thiel, C. "What MIS Needs to Know about Strategic Planning." *Info Systems* 31 (August 1989): 38–40.

Thompson, T. "Scanning Tomorrow's Banking Environment." *U.S. Banker* 8 (November 1987): 79–80.

Timberman, E. "If You Don't Position Your Bank the Competition Will." *Bank Marketing* 17 (February 1985): 10–12.

Timberman, E. "Positioning to Maximize Results." *Banks In Insurance Report* 1 (March 1986): 4–7.

Van Art, R. "Strategic Planning in Trust." *Trust Management Update* (October 1985): 15–18.

Vecchiot, R. "Change: How Banks Can Manage and Still Survive." *Mid-Continent Banker* 81 (June 1985): 46–48.

Wade, A. "Developing a National Presence (Bank of Boston)." *U.S. Banker* 96 (February 1985): 48–51.

Walter, Ingo. *Deregulating Wall Street: Commercial Bank Penetration of the Corporate Securities Market.* New York: Wiley, 1985.

White, S. "When Short-Term Goals Conflict with the Big Picture." *Bank Systems & Equipment* 26 (June 1989): 68–69.

Whitehead, D., and Gup, B. "Bank & Thrift Profitability: Does Strategic Planning Really Pay?" *Federal Reserve Bank of Atlanta: Economic Review Press* 70 (October 1985): 14–25.

Whittle, J. "Criteria for Judging Your Bank's Preparedness for the Future." *American Banker* 149 (April 1984): 4.

Willax, P. "Planning for the Future Requires an Understanding of the Past." *American Banker* 151 (December 1986): 4+.

Willax, P. "Follow-Through Is as Important as Calling the Shot (marketing management)." *American Banker* 153 (October 1988): 4+

Wright, Don. *The Effective Bank Director*. Reston, Va.: Reston Publishing Company, 1985.

Zwick, C. "Planning for Expansion in a Changing Banking Environment." *Issues in Bank Regulation* 8 (Autumn 1984): 11–15.

INDEX

Index note to the reader: Tables are indicated by the numbers in bold print.

ABOUT THE AUTHORS

Douglas V. Austin, Ph.D., JD, CFA, is President and CEO of Austin Financial Services, Inc., a financial institution consulting firm specializing in mergers and acquisitions, bank and branch purchases and sales, investment banking, and bank director/management education, including strategic planning, and profitability and capital planning.

Dr. Austin is author of 15 books, including *The Community Bank Survival Guide* and *Financial Institution Director Liabilities and Responsibilities,* and over 500 articles. He taught at Indiana University and the University of Michigan before becoming an economist with the Federal Reserve Bank of Cleveland. He subsequently taught at Western Michigan University before becoming Chairman and Professor of Finance of the Department of Finance at the University of Toledo. Dr. Austin is currently Professor Emeritus of the Department of Finance at the University of Toledo.

Craig D. Bernard is Executive Vice President for Austin Financial Services, Inc., involved with consulting for community banks and thrifts. A Bachelor of Science graduate in Finance from Indiana University, Mr. Bernard received his MBA from the University of Toledo, was employed by Bank One Corporation, and served as a consultant for Austin Associates before joining Austin Financial Services, Inc., in 1989. His expertise is mergers and acquisitions, bank and branch purchases and sales, strategic planning, and bank stock valuation. Mr. Bernard participates on a regular basis with Dr. Austin in conferences, workshops, seminars, and professional presentations concerning management and director education for community banks and thrifts.